The Value of Debt

The Value of Debt

*How to Manage Both Sides
of Your Balance Sheet
to Maximize Wealth*

Thomas J. Anderson

WILEY

Published by John Wiley & Sons, Inc., Hoboken, New Jersey.
Published simultaneously in Canada.

For general information on our other products and services or for technical support, please contact our Customer Care Department within the United States at (800) 762-2974, outside the United States at (317) 572-3993 or fax (317) 572-4002.

Wiley publishes in a variety of print and electronic formats and by print-on-demand. Some material included with standard print versions of this book may not be included in e-books or in print-on-demand. If this book refers to media such as a CD or DVD that is not included in the version you purchased, you may download this material at http://booksupport.wiley.com. For more information about Wiley products, visit www.wiley.com.

Library of Congress Cataloging-in-Publication Data:

Anderson, Thomas J. (Certified investment management analyst)
    The value of debt : how to manage both sides of a balance sheet to maximize wealth / Thomas J. Anderson, CIMA, CRPC.
      pages cm
    Includes bibliographical references and index.
    ISBN 978-1-118-75861-8 (hardback); ISBN 978-1-118-75851-9 (ebk);
    ISBN 978-1-118-75863-2 (ebk)
      1. Finance, Personal. 2. Debt. I. Title.
    HG179.A55976   2013
    332.024'02—dc23

                                                                    2013020675

Printed in the United States of America

10 9 8 7 6 5 4 3 2 1

For Sarah, John, Rosemary, and Oliver

Contents

Foreword

C hange is the one constant in the financial services industry. In 1970, there were many days where trading volume on the New York Stock Exchange did not exceed 10 million shares. Recently, there have been multiple days with over 5 billion shares traded, an increase of 500 times. We have seen the development of integrated money market accounts, explosive growth in mutual funds, and the proliferation of such instruments as exchange-traded funds, separately managed accounts, hedge funds, private equity, structured products, and managed futures for commodities. This is taking place not just in the United States but across the world.

With time, advice has evolved as well. It had to. Clients have more investment choices than ever before. The global economy has become more interconnected and global capital markets have gone through explosive growth in both size and depth. The financial services industry has listened to the demands of its clients and responded accordingly. Investors today have the opportunity to invest in more asset classes through more vehicles in more places around the world than ever before.

So, where do we go from here? I had the opportunity to visit with Tom Anderson while he was putting together this book and he pointed out a glaring omission that I believe holds true for most all of us: throughout his primary school years, college education, graduate school, and professional life, Tom had not been educated as to the virtues of correctly structured debt. One can fill a library with books on debt strategies and capital structures for corporations, but there is virtually no material on the subject for individuals or families. Why? As I reflected on this some more, I found it shocking that there is not more material, education, debate, and discussion on this topic.

The financial industry has largely treated debt as though it were an outside force, considered and controlled independently of the rest of an individual's financial life. But who has not used a mortgage to finance a home, obtained a student loan to cover college tuition, or borrowed to buy a new car? It seems common sense to treat these moments of capital acquisition holistically, as part of an overall financial plan. However, this happens all too infrequently in practice. While most financial firms and advisors today are able to deliver integrated solutions by and large, they are not yet delivering integrated advice.

Most advisors give sound advice when it comes to equity but overlook the other half of the balance sheet. Getting sound advice on liability management can be critical especially during those first years of retirement. Tom has written a must-read book for anyone looking to make better financial decisions. This book should be a staple for Financial Advisors who want to do a complete job of advising their clients.

Tom's background, at some of the top schools in finance in the United States and abroad, combined with his experience in investment banking and as a financial advisor, affords him a unique perspective to address this gap. His ideas come together in this book to deliver a new perspective that represents a substantial step forward toward a cohesive solution.

The excesses of debt and reckless lending at the heart of our recent financial crisis have been well documented. This is no reason to ignore debt as an effective financial arrow in your quiver. In fact, it's all the more reason to approach debt in an intelligent and educated fashion. What's true about investing is that it entails risk, yet can offer rewards. The same principle applies to a debt philosophy.

The ideas expressed in this book may or may not be appropriate for your individual situation. The most important contribution of this work is that it should create more questions than answers. These questions in turn should lead to quality, holistic conversations about all aspects of your financial life with your tax, legal, and financial advisors. Change is constant, but as the book describes, with integrated, holistic advice we can be better prepared for this change, and for the future ahead.

Robert D. Knapp
President
Supernova Consulting Group
Author of *The Supernova Advisor: Crossing the Invisible Bridge to Exceptional Client Service and Consistent Growth*

Acknowledgments

This book is an amalgamation of all aspects of my education and career. I wish to thank my many professors at Washington University and The University of Chicago—you have greatly influenced this work. To Professor Jaffe from the Wharton School of Business, I'll never forget the CIMA final exam, and I hope you see how often your textbook is cited in the endnotes, for those who want additional detail on corporate finance.

My coworkers from my time in investment banking in wealth management inspire me; I have learned from each of you.

Carl Klaus defined *the value of debt* as the unique idea to develop into this book. His advice and guidance have been invaluable. Molly Chehak taught me about the process of creating a book and the publishing industry.

Phil Burrelle, I appreciate your modeling assistance. John Osako and team at Informatics, thank you for your amazing technical support.

Rafe Sagalyn, you are an outstanding agent, and I sincerely appreciate your guidance. David Zylstra and Denny Redmond, I value your advice and counsel.

Jordan S. Gruber turned my initial ideas and writing forays into an actual publishable manuscript, and I can't thank him enough for his incredible efforts. He is an artist and helped me express complicated ideas in an easy to understand language. RJ, I am so grateful that you introduced us.

I would like to thank the following readers for their thoughtful and insightful advice: Greg Boester, Alex Dunlap, Jim Harris, Dr. Curt Hass, Kate Hladky, Jim Hoffman, John Huey, Dave and Patricia Knuth, Randy Kurtz, Chris Merker, Eliot Protsch, Dr. Jerry Shirk, Dick Siders, Julianne Smith, Nathan Swanson, and Steve Vanourny. The book is a better book because of you.

To the incredible team at Wiley; thank you for all of your support through the development and production phases of this book. Tula Batanchiev has been my North Star and guided me through every step. Judy Howarth, my development editor and Melissa Lopez, my production editor were invaluable to me; I appreciate their superb editorial skills. Any remaining mistakes are my own.

Mom, thanks for sending me to Wall Street Camp when I was 16; I wouldn't be in the industry without you. I value your advice and treasure your love and support.

I would particularly like to thank my team: Kerry Abdoney, Jon Bancks, Stacey Halyard, Darla Lowe, JoAnn Masters, Fred Rose, Julie Vogt, and summer analyst Ben Rees. You not only made tremendous contributions to this book, but also enabled me to dedicate time to writing this while maintaining growth and excellence within our practice.

Kids, I love who you are and who you are becoming. I am proud to be your father. You give me more joy than I ever thought was possible.

Sarah, you are an incredible partner in every aspect of my life. None of this would be possible without you. You make me a better person and I enjoy life more because of you. I love you.

Introduction

Who is this book for? This book is *not* for everybody. To make best use of it, there are three prerequisites, as follows:

1. First, you should *have an open mind*.
2. Second, you should probably *be working with a progressive, holistic financial advisor or private banker who also has an open mind* and who can help you implement the strategies, practices, and tactics that will be suggested here. (If you happen to be a financial advisor or private banker, then please consider the book as being meant for you too, as well as for your appropriate clients. The ideas found here may help you do a much better job for at least some of them.)
3. Third—and this is either something that will be true for you at this point or may be true for you at some point in the future—*you will need to have sufficient investible assets to implement these ideas.* "Sufficient assets" is intentionally vague. Initially the book was written specifically for Accredited Investors (particularly those with a net worth of more than $1 million, excluding their primary residence) and you should approach the material with this in mind. However every situation is unique and you will have to work with

your advisors to see if these ideas are appropriate for you and your family based on your assets, income, goals, and objectives.

Now, if you don't yet have sufficient investable assets, you very likely will still find many of the ideas useful and interesting, and something to aim at incorporating into your financial life over time. However, *many of the book's concepts and principles simply cannot be effectively applied to individuals without a high enough net worth*. In fact, many of the ideas could have a very negative effect if used by lower net worth individuals, particularly if the concepts are misapplied. Nonetheless, if you aren't yet part of the target market for this book but you find the ideas interesting, please see Appendix B, "Strategic Debt Practice for the Young and Those with Limited Assets," where we discuss how you can use the ideas found here as a frame for your thinking and a guide to your actions.

In general, then, *the real sweet spot* for making use of the ideas, principles, and practices found in this book is individuals and families who

- Have sufficient investible assets.
- Want to position their lives so that they can retire in relative comfort.
- Are committed to taking care of their family members for the long run regardless of what type of emergency or natural disaster might arrive.
- Are interested in minimizing the taxes they pay or in buying a second home or other substantial assets in a much better way.

Assuming that you are part of the audience this book was written for, the next question is *how you can most effectively make use of the ideas found here*? This brings us to the question of what this book is . . . and what it is not.

Simply put, *this book is a general guide*. It will show you how to take on and make intelligent use of an optimal amount of Strategic Debt by comprehensively and holistically managing both sides of your balance sheet, that is, both your debts and your assets. *What this book is not, however, is a detailed how-to guide for implementing the ideas found here*. As already stated in this section, if you are going to move forward with the ideas in this book, you should almost certainly consult with a knowledgeable financial advisor or private banker who can not only help you do things in the best way possible, but also make sure that the ideas found here are actually appropriate for you.

Even the most risk averse individuals—those with the lowest risk tolerances and the least ability to psychologically or financially absorb an unexpected shock—may benefit from the ideas in this book. At a minimum such individuals may want to seriously consider putting an assets-based loan facility, or ABLF, in place, as we'll get to briefly.

Why might the ideas found here *not* be appropriate for you even if you fall into the target market defined previously? Well, life is risky, and risk and reward are directly interrelated. So even though we feel that the ideas and practices you'll find here may tend to systematically reduce your risk and may make you wealthier in the long run in a number of ways, you still have to keep in mind that things could change, these ideas could backfire, or they may not be right for you. *To this point, Appendix C is perhaps the most important part of this book—it is an absolute must read.* In an earlier draft this appendix was called "All of the reasons the ideas in this book can be bad for you."

In addition to this appendix it is important that you read the endnotes in each section where additional risks and topics for discussion with your advisors are identified. In the interest of not having multiple disclaimers and risk factors repeating over and over throughout the book, we have packed a lot of important information about risk into the appendix and endnotes, so please pay close attention to both of them. Accordingly, it is important to know that all of the ideas in this book go together. You can't just pick up this book and read one part of it. This includes, but is not limited to, the discussion of risks and disclaimers throughout the book. It is all interconnected and it all goes together. The material is presented with a goal of encouraging thoughtful conversation and rigorous debate on the risks and potential benefits of the concepts between you and your advisors.

Not about Buying What You Can't Afford, but about Strategy

It is essential to know that this book is not about buying things you cannot afford. It is about better ways to finance and pay for the things that you can afford.

Once, after I gave a presentation, some people came up to me afterward and said, "So your goal is to have everybody take on a lot of debt?"

That is *not* the objective of this book. Instead, the intent is to express ideas and concepts as to what is *optimal*, and to encourage people to have a strategy around their debt. Too often people either have way too much debt or they are completely debt averse and have too little debt. There is an optimal middle ground, and the purpose of this book is therefore to set forth a reasonable framework for having an optimal debt strategy.

The Book's Real Goal

The specific strategies outlined in this book may, in fact, not be optimal for your particular situation. However, the ideas found here should help lay the foundation for you to create your own personalized, optimized debt philosophy. In a certain sense then, *the real goal of this particular book is to challenge your basic assumptions and beliefs about the wise and strategic use of debt.* Ideally, if the book is successful, it will raise many more questions than it answers, questions you should investigate—with regard to your own situation—with your tax, legal, and financial advisors.

In the eyes of its author, however, this book will be considered a success if by the time you are done reading it, some or all of the following have happened:

- You choose to have some debt at all points in your life.
- You choose to *not* aggressively pay down debt in the years leading up to retirement.
- You choose to a much greater degree how much tax you will pay the government when you are retired (versus having the government tell you how much tax you need to pay).
- You think about and monitor your optimal debt ratio and how it changes over time.
- You think about ways to reduce the costs, impact level, and duration of any potential financial distress.
- You have more questions than answers.

WHY I WROTE THIS BOOK

Dear Reader,

Throughout the book I occasionally take the liberty of speaking to you more directly and informally. For example, right now I wanted to briefly let you know exactly *why* I wrote this book in the first place, which is actually quite simple.

I have been teaching the ideas and practices you'll find here for a number of years now. Excited and even somewhat amazed by the *value of debt*—how to strategically use one's Indebted Strengths to be in a much better long-term position—I have been asked many times for a detailed treatment of these ideas.

Well, I looked high and low, both online and offline, and couldn't find one, so I felt that given the incredible value that people are already finding in these ideas, I would go ahead and take the plunge and do my best to write it all up in an easy-to-understand book (although you will still need—and most certainly will want—the help of the right financial advisor to fully understand or implement any specific actions).

Structurally the book starts out by laying the foundation for a solid Strategic Debt Philosophy. It then transitions to understanding a key building block, which is the incredible benefit of having an asset-based loan facility at your disposal. With these tools in place, I then explore scenarios for success and present specific case studies.

A solid foundation is essential to all things in life, but it is particularly necessary with respect to formulating and implementing a Strategic Debt Philosophy. I would encourage you to not skip ahead to the case studies regardless of your level of education or familiarity with the subject.

Case studies are complicated in a book such as this. The material is difficult to understand without examples but there is risk that somebody could look at a simple example and try to apply that to their complex life. Individual situations are unique and multifaceted. It is worth noting that all case studies presented in

(*Continued*)

WHY I WROTE THIS BOOK (*Continued*)

this book are for educational and illustrative purposes only and should be used to help trigger meaningful conversations with your advisors about your individual situation. They cannot be—and are not intended to be—advice that you can directly apply to your situation. There are many risks to these ideas, and, of course, all loans are subject to eligibility and approval by the lender.

Because of the risks involved, I can't stress enough the importance of reading the appendixes and endnotes, stress-testing your philosophy, and becoming as prepared as possible for a wide range of outcomes. Moreover, never underestimate the importance, necessity, and value of working with an outstanding group of professional advisors to implement these ideas according to your individual needs, goals, financial condition, and risk tolerance.

Some readers will undoubtedly desire more detail than a book such as this can provide and still be appealing to general readers. If you have an academic or financial background, you will find that this book's theoretical basis can be found in finance and accounting materials that are taught in graduate and undergraduate business courses throughout the world. You will also recognize that several of the most famous theories in finance are directly or indirectly referenced. In order to keep the material appealing to readers of all levels, however, most technical finance references have been placed in the endnotes.

A quick note on interest rates and the global economy will also be helpful at this point. The ideas expressed in this book are designed to transcend political borders and to transcend time. Clearly, over multiple countries and multiple economic conditions, the range of outcomes we will see in our lifetimes may be vast. In the text I use interest rates that represent the current economic environment, but these ideas could have been applied equally in 1980. I've done my best to be world neutral, but there are a number of U.S. specific references, particularly as to taxes. Many of these ideas can be applied around the world

(*Continued*)

and in multiple economic environments. Accordingly, regardless of where you live, a good exercise would be to imagine "what if" you applied these concepts to the United States in the 1970s, France in the 1920s, England in the 1960s, Japan in the 2000s, and Argentina in the 1990s.

I hope you find a great deal of value in these pages and that they inspire you to create and implement your own Strategic Debt Philosophy.

—Tom Anderson

Part 1

THE VALUE OF DEBT IN THE MANAGEMENT OF WEALTH

Ignorance is the curse of God; knowledge is the wing wherewith we fly to heaven.

—*William Shakespeare,* Henry VI, *Part 2*

1

Chapter 1

Strategic Debt Philosophy: An Overview

How This Book Can Add Value to Your Life

This book aims to bring forth a new vision of the value of debt in the management of individual and family wealth. On the one hand, virtually every company already looks at both sides of its balance sheet—assets and debts—and consciously strives to come up with an optimal debt ratio.[1] On the other hand, the vast majority of individuals, wealthy or not, *are either dramatically overleveraged (have too much debt) or, at the other extreme, are substantially underleveraged (have no debt at all).*[2] Those in this second camp typically hold the notion that debt is always bad, should almost always be avoided, and if taken on, should be paid off as soon as humanly possible.

There is a reason, however, why practically all companies acknowledge the value of debt and seek to have an optimal debt ratio in place.[3] Simply put, by strategically taking on and managing debt, these companies realize that they can take advantage of what we'll call the *Indebted Strengths* that come along with that debt, which, as we'll describe shortly, include Increased Liquidity, Increased Flexibility, Increased Leverage, and Increased Survivability.

As it turns out, despite the general antidebt knee-jerk reaction that most people have, many wealthy individuals and families—from the moderately affluent to the ultra-affluent—can also make use of these Indebted Strengths to their own substantial long-term advantage. For starters—in later chapters I will get into the details on all of these and more—the strategic use of debt can help enable you and your family to do the following:

- Quickly come up with the funds needed to respond to natural disasters, health crises, or personal difficulties of nearly any kind.
- Generate tax-efficient income in retirement (and potentially access your money tax free).
- Purchase a second home in a much less expensive manner.
- Become progressively wealthier by "capturing the spread" between the cost of debt and the return on investment that you can likely generate through appropriate low-risk investing strategies.

The Five Tenets (or Action Principles) of Strategic Debt Philosophy

There are five tenets—or action principles—that form the core of Strategic Debt Philosophy:

1. Adopt a Holistic—Not Atomistic—Approach
2. Explore Thinking and Acting Like a Company
3. Understand Limitations on Commonly Held Views of Personal Debt
4. Set Your Sights on an Optimal Personal Debt Ratio
5. Stay Open-Minded, Ask Questions, and Verify What Works

Each of the five action principles is expressed as a kind of injunction, starting with words like *adopt*, *explore*, and *understand*—words that tell you to *do* something specific. This is done to let you know that while this may be a chapter on the *philosophy* of Strategic Debt, it is not meant to be a vague, head-in-the-clouds type of exercise. There is real work—internal thinking and questioning, consulting first with one's spouse and family members and then with one's professional advisors—that is absolutely necessary before going forward with any of the specific Strategic Debt Practices recommended in this book. Let's, then, now turn to the five tenets.

First Tenet: Adopt a Holistic (Comprehensive)—Not Atomistic—Approach

The first tenet of Strategic Debt Philosophy—and for that matter, the first tenet of all true wealth management philosophies—is to adopt a *holistic* approach. Merriam-Webster.com defines holistic as "Relating to or concerned with wholes or with complete systems rather than with the analysis of, treatment of, or dissection into parts." Similarly, TheFreeDictionary.com defines holistic as "Emphasizing the importance of the whole and the interdependence of its parts."

For purposes of this book, the terms *holistic* and *comprehensive* will be treated as synonymous. A holistic wealth management approach, then, is one that goes far beyond the typical investment portfolio approach. Instead, it starts with the needs, goals, and dreams of an individual or family, then looks not only at their immediate financial situation but also the entirety of their wealth, and then takes into account everything from estate and retirement planning to taxes and insurance to end-of-life concerns (health care, residency, medical powers of attorney, etc.), and then, finally, methodically backs out cash-flow needs and projections.

What's important about a holistic approach is that it doesn't separate analysis and action into atomistic silos, where decisions on everything from buying a car to making long-term investments are made without taking into account the impacts and effects of that decision on the entirety of an individual's or family's wealth. A holistic approach does its best to take everything into account (as well as how everything interacts with everything else) and does so on many levels, from the most general to the most detailed. This often means calling in experts—like high-level tax accountants, lawyers, insurance experts, and so on—to ensure that the best possible informed choices are made.

Adopting a holistic—and not atomistic or fragmented—approach to the value of debt has a number of consequences and implications. First, it brings to the table the critical importance of looking at both assets *and* debts, as we'll continue to explore throughout this chapter and the rest of this book. Second, without a holistic approach to wealth management that does indeed take into account both assets and debts, it is very difficult if not impossible to adopt and follow through on a holistic wealth management philosophy overall. That is, thoughtfully considering and factoring in everything that is known about debt, as well as what is known about assets, is essential to deriving maximum value from a comprehensive wealth management approach. Finally, a holistic approach to Strategic Debt Philosophy enables the exploration of the four Indebted Strengths that will be explored in detail in Chapter 2.

Second Tenet: Explore Thinking and Acting Like a Company

According to *Corporate Finance* (Ross, Westerfield, and Jaffe 2013),

> The goal of financial management is to make money or add value for the owners.[4]

A company is generally focused on gaining profits. That is, with the exception of nonprofit and not-for-profit companies, in the vast majority of cases the raison d'être—reason for being—of a company is to do well financially.[5] One would think, then, that when it comes to money, companies would tend to know what they are doing, which is one reason why it's important for wealthy individuals and families to explore thinking and acting the way that companies do.

One objection to thinking and acting like a company may be that, indeed, individuals and families are *not* companies, and their main purpose is *not* to gain profits. While that's quite true, it's also true that the exploration of thinking and acting like a company can have many benefits for individuals and families. Importantly, companies are often much more objective about financial-related matters than are individuals and families. So while their ultimate goals may differ, there is a lot of good learning that can come from exploring how companies think and what they do. Put differently, while you as an individual or family may not be primarily focused on making a profit, you nonetheless constitute an organized system of inputs and outputs that absolutely relies on having sufficient financial resources at the ready in order to get on with "the business of life."

A related factor is that companies have specialized financial leaders—chief financial officers, or CFOs—who are very clear about what does and doesn't work in the financial realm.[6] Much training, much education, and much knowledge about best practices reside within these individuals. If the vast majority of CFOs follow a particular practice, you can bet there's a good reason why.

A second objection to thinking and acting like a company can also be raised: In the pursuit of profits, companies may ultimately be much more willing to go bankrupt than you, as an individual or family, are willing to take a chance on. That is, for the most part, companies are so ultimately focused on making a profit that they engage in certain types of behaviors that you, as an individual or family, might not be willing to risk. This may or may not be true and it still doesn't mean that there aren't some huge lessons to be learned from at least the simple exploration of thinking and acting like a company.

Now that we've looked at the general reasons and objections as to why you could explore thinking and acting like a company, let's turn toward what it is, in particular, that sets companies apart in the realm of a holistic approach to Strategic Debt Philosophy. First, and most importantly, consider the following true proposition:

Virtually every company of any size chooses a holistic approach to its balance sheet that embraces having both assets and debts.[7]

In fact, as of this writing, there are four U.S. publicly traded companies that have a AAA rating (and even they use different forms of debt!).[8] This is not because there aren't many companies that are big enough and wealthy enough to pay off their debt entirely. (Could Coca-Cola, Walmart, or Procter & Gamble, for example, pay off all of their debt if they wanted to? Of course they could . . . but they don't, and they won't.) Instead, it's because *companies—which are all about doing well financially—consciously choose to have an optimal amount of debt.*

Yes, they are mindful of how much debt they have and how that debt is structured, but they take on debt and keep debt on their balance sheet *on purpose.* They do this so they can make use of what I will later define as their various Indebted Strengths, that is, to increase their liquidity, the amount of capital they have to work with, their long-term survivability, and so on. Companies, then, go out of their way not just to embrace debt where it is useful—for example, by issuing debt to buy back more of the company's publicly traded stock—but to determine and make use of their optimal debt ratio, that is, the optimal ratio between their assets and their debts.[9]

A great deal of research has gone into what the optimal debt ratio is for companies. As Eugene Brigham and Joel Houston explain in *Fundamentals of Financial Management* (2004), "The optimal capital structure must strike a balance between risk and return so as to maximize the firm's stock price." In just a little while, we'll discuss what average company debt ratios tend to actually look like in the real world.[10]

If you think about it, there is no question that shareholders of all companies want, need, and expect their companies to be successful. Proper design and implementation of the company's capital structure—and their overall debt philosophy—is a key part of these expectations. Interestingly, there are some theories out there that say companies should be almost 99 percent debt and 1 percent equity![11] Nobel Prizes have been awarded for the theories with respect to corporate finance and the optimal corporate capital structure. It is important that we are familiar with that work and consider its potential implications on our personal lives.

If you are a CFO of a public company and you haven't focused on your optimal debt ratio, do you know what you could be?

That's right: You could be fired!

Consider, then, for a moment, what the role of the CFO in a company is. He or she starts by taking a *holistic* approach to the company's balance sheet. This begins by considering the corporation's total assets and the likelihood of the company encountering financial distress, along with what the fallout of that financial distress would be in terms of direct and indirect costs, the impact level of that financial distress, and its duration. (See Chapter 2 for a description of these terms and dynamics.)

With all this in mind, the CFO then determines the cash flow needs of the organization, and then looks at how much debt the company should have in terms of accessing the indebted strengths of Increased Liquidity, Flexibility, Leverage, and Survivability. Structuring the right amount of debt in the right way is critical, because if the company takes on too much risk in the form of increased debt then it could go bankrupt. If it doesn't take on enough of the right kind of debt then it may not be maximizing value and/or may increase the chances of either running into a liquidity crisis or being bought out by a hostile party. It's not surprising, then, that most companies have fairly constant debt ratios from year to year (as opposed to individuals, who tend to either have way too much debt or who want to pay off all of their debt as soon as they can).[12]

If companies are willing, able, and deeply committed to embracing Strategic Debt Philosophy and Practice, then you, as a natural, real, live person or head of a family, should be willing to at least work with your advisors to explore the potential benefits—and risks—of these ideas as well.

Companies and their CFOs, then, spend a lot of time—a whole lot of time in a holistic frame of mind—thinking all of this through. The big take-away here, then, is that there is an incredible disconnect between something that almost all companies do and something that far too few wealthy individuals and families do or are even willing to think about.

As previously stated, individuals clearly are not corporations. It would be extreme to say that they are the same, and it would be equally extreme to say that they have nothing in common. Our goal is to explore that white space in the middle.

SOMETHING ELSE THAT COMPANIES DO THAT YOU COULD, TOO

While we're going to school on financially motivated companies and how they think and act, we should point out that there is something else that companies do that you could probably do as well: Avoid amortization whenever possible.

One hundred percent of all debt issued by publicly traded American corporations is issued on an interest-only basis.[13]

If I buy a bond from GE or Coca-Cola (or any other large corporation), I will receive interest payments only (the bond coupon). The only time I will receive a principal payment will be at call date or maturity. Why is it that all corporate debt is interest only but many individuals amortize their cars, their houses, and so on?

As we will explore later, and as CFOs already know, having *any* required payments on your debt decreases your flexibility and ultimately increases your risk of and cost of financial distress.

Third Tenet: Understand Limitations on Commonly Held Views of Personal Debt

How can we understand this "incredible disconnect" between how companies holistically think about their balance sheets and how the great majority of individuals tend to never think this way? It all begins with the perception that popular culture has of debt. For example, consider the words of the great William Shakespeare, who in his play *Hamlet* has Lord Polonius say,

Neither a borrower nor a lender be;
For loan oft loses both itself and friend,
And borrowing dulls the edge of husbandry.

Basically, debt has a terrible reputation. "I'm an accumulator; no debt for me," you might hear someone you respect say. Or perhaps you had a grandparent or other family member say, "When I die, I want to die debt free so I can pass my wealth, not my obligations, on to my children or grandchildren." Or you might know some fiercely independent person who has told you, time and again, that they don't want anyone—least of all a bank or financial institution—having "anything over me."

This general, sweeping, negative view of debt can also be found in financial articles and books written for individuals and families. As part of putting this book together, an in-depth online research effort was conducted to assess whether Strategic Debt Philosophy and Practices were fairly evaluated and considered. After wading through many online articles that simply focus on the best way to restructure and get rid of debt as soon as possible, about 20 online articles were discovered that had something positive to say about debt.

Mainly, these 20 or so articles discussed the difference between *good debt* (for example, taking on debt for educational purposes or to buy a house—a subject we'll return to later on) and *bad debt* (for example, credit card debt). None of these articles—not a single one—recommended that wealthy individuals and families investigate the idea of attaining an optimal debt ratio throughout their lives. Instead, the simplistic idea that all debt is bad kept popping up, and the importance of eventually getting rid of all debt showed up time and time again.

What we are facing, then, is a knee-jerk antidebt reaction—ingrained aversion to debt. In a certain sense, this makes sense, because many people are *either totally debt averse* (either have no debt at all or have the goal of having no debt at all) or *have way too much debt* and are overleveraged and have therefore put themselves at an increased risk of financial distress. Those who see others getting into trouble have their prejudice against all debt in all circumstances reinforced. Similarly, as some of the concepts in this book may at first seem unusual, counterintuitive, or even controversial, it is easy to see why a quick look might just serve to further fan the flames of the all-debt-is-bad perspective.

> The real problem, then, is the lack of education that almost everyone has about the use of Strategic Debt.

The lack of education has been compounded by strong antidebt prejudices that have been reinforced throughout popular culture for centuries. While it may be true that for many individuals debt should be avoided like the plague, it's just as certainly true that a wealthy individual or family can intelligently take advantage of the Indebted Strengths that come from taking on the right kind of debt and achieving an optimal debt ratio.[14]

In short, *most popular views on debt are extremely limited.* They don't consider how a wealthy individual or family can greatly benefit from the right kind of debt. They don't consider the value of thinking and acting like a company in appropriate circumstances, and they don't explore the Indebted Strengths that come hand in hand when strategically taking on appropriate debt.

Instead, they simply rely on the knee-jerk reaction that most people have toward debt, as if all people taking on debt were the same and all types of debt were the same. By understanding these limitations on popularly held notions of debt, you can free your mind, shed your prejudices, and begin the investigation of whether the ideas and practices suggested here might make sense and be appropriate for you and your family.

Fourth Tenet: Set Your Sights on an Optimal Personal Debt Ratio

One premise of this book is that when it comes to an ideal debt ratio, there is an optimal sweet spot for individuals, just like there is for companies, and that those of us who can afford to do so should most certainly be targeting that sweet spot. As pointed out earlier, there tend to be two types of people: those who are very highly leveraged and take on way too much debt and those who are totally debt adverse and don't have any debt whatsoever.

If, however, you have considered (or better yet, have already accepted and adopted) the first three tenets of Strategic Debt Philosophy—adopt a holistic approach, explore thinking and acting like a company, understand limitations on commonly held views of debt—then you are ready to at least consider adopting the fourth tenet, which is to set your sights on an optimal personal debt ratio.

You see, there is so much antidebt loading in our culture and society that even the idea that there is—or might be—something called an optimal personal debt ratio is quite foreign to most people, even those who work in the world of finance. But once you have understood that there is in fact an ideal debt ratio—or an ideal range—for you (and your family) to personally target, you can go about doing what it takes to achieve that ideal ratio or target range. Exactly what that range is will be discussed in the next chapter on Strategic Debt Practices.

> Setting your sights on achieving that ideal ratio makes it far more likely that you will achieve it.

In Chapter 3 I discuss how to examine your balance sheet to determine your current debt ratio, how your debt ratio may change over time, and some of the ironies that are involved with attaining optimal debt ratios, for example, those who are at the greatest risk of financial distress are also the ones who can benefit the most from their Indebted Strengths. The key point here, though, is to understand that there is indeed such a thing as an optimal debt ratio for wealthy individuals and families, and that if you don't yet understand how strategic debt can benefit you, then you are unlikely to ever obtain this ideal ratio.

WHEN DETERMINING YOUR IDEAL DEBT RATIO REALLY HITS HOME

There is a big issue that needs to be considered when approaching the value of debt and setting one's sights on an ideal debt ratio. That issue involves whether one should own one's home free and clear, as well as exactly how to calculate one's debt ratio with regard to this. This issue will be returned to in some detail when I show you how to calculate your debt ratio.

For now, let's just acknowledge that some people feel very strongly that they should indeed own their primary residence free and clear, and that while this belief is justifiable, it is not mutually exclusive with respect to many of the ideas found in this book.

Fifth Tenet: Stay Open-Minded, Ask Questions, and Verify What Works

In the introduction the following statement was made:

> The real goal of this particular book is to challenge your basic assumptions and beliefs about the wise use of debt.

The fifth tenet or action principle, then, is all about thinking, questioning, and verifying the ideas and practices that have been presented in this book. Even if something looks like a great idea, don't necessarily assume it is true or appropriate for you and your family or will work in your situation.

On the one hand, then, you want to stay as open-minded as you can. On the other hand, you want to be relentless in your questioning, your inquiries, and your determination as to whether any particular practice laid out in this book is the right thing for you to do. Whether any particular practice or action is what works in your case will take some investigation and discernment, so please be willing to put on your thinking cap and take the time to really understand your situation and what is being suggested.

Chapter 1: Summary and Checklist

This chapter described the five tenets—or action principles—that taken together constitute Strategic Debt Philosophy. The first tenet, which is "Adopt a Holistic (Comprehensive)—Not Atomistic—Approach," says that you should look at Strategic Debt Philosophy, as well as everything concerning the management of your wealth, in a complete, comprehensive, big picture manner.

The second tenet, "Explore Thinking and Acting Like a Company," asks you to consider why nearly all companies embrace a holistic approach to their balance sheets, one that consciously optimizes the amount of debt that a company has. The third tenet, "Understand Limitations on Commonly Held Views of Personal Debt," considers popularly held—and almost universally negative—views on debt. It also reviews the research that was done in preparation for writing this book, research that shows that the idea that "all debt is ultimately bad" is pervasive in online articles and that, to our knowledge, no previous book has comprehensively addressed this subject matter.

The fourth tenet—"Set Your Sights on an Optimal Personal Debt Ratio"—considers the value of understanding and then being guided by an optimal debt-to-assets ratio, first for companies and then for individuals and families. Finally, the fifth tenet concerns the nature of practical knowledge generally, and strongly advises you to "Stay Open-Minded, Ask Questions, and Verify What Works" in your particular situation.[15]

Checklist

☐ Does the first tenet—adopt a holistic approach—make sense to you?

☐ Do you understand the value of exploring thinking and acting like a company does, as the second tenet suggests?

☐ Were you surprised to learn that virtually every U.S. company of any size consciously optimizes its balance sheet, that is, takes on debt on purpose?

☐ Can you see how popular culture reinforces the notion that all debt is bad, as per the third tenet?

☐ Does setting your sights on achieving an optimal personal debt ratio—as the fourth tenet suggests—make sense to you? Do you intend to at least look into your own debt ratio to see whether it is optimal?

☐ Are you committed to the action steps stated in the fifth tenet: stay open-minded, ask questions, and verify what works in your own situation in consultation with your family members and professional advisors?

Notes

1. Stephen A. Ross, Randolph Westerfield, and Jeffrey Jaffe, *Corporate Finance*, 10th ed. (New York: McGraw-Hill, 2013). Pages 494–525 address this subject in detail.

2. www.federalreserve.gov/econresdata/scf/files/2010_SCF_Chartbook.pdf provides great insight into the general trends of individuals. This specific

statement is also derived from surveys, the collective experience of my team, and the experience of the bankers I have worked with throughout my career.

3. According to John Graham and Campbell Harvey, "The Theory and Practice of Corporate Finance," *Journal of Financial Economics*, May/June 2011, most firms employ target debt-equity ratios. Only 19 percent of the firms avoid target debt ratios. Results elsewhere in the paper indicate that large firms are more likely than small firms to employ these targets. Ten percent have a very strict target; 34 percent have a somewhat tight target/range; 37 percent have a flexible target; and 19 percent have no target ratio or range.

4. Ross, Westerfield, and Jaffe, *Corporate Finance*, 11. The text continues with a discussion on profit maximization as the most commonly cited goal. Multiple goals of a corporation clearly exist, such as survive; avoid financial distress and bankruptcy; beat the competition; maximize sales of market share; minimize costs; maximize profits; maintain steady earnings growth. The text also explains that the goals fall into two primary classes: profitability and controlling risk/avoiding bankruptcy.

5. Even nonprofit organizations have a goal of not losing money. It is outside of the scope of this book to go into detail on nonprofit objectives and their use of debt, but we can safely say that many nonprofits have CFOs and many use debt strategies similar to the ideas expressed in this book.

6. Ross, Westerfield, and Jaffe, *Corporate Finance*, 2. "Finance can be thought of as the study of the following three questions: (1) "In what long lived assets should the firm invest? This question concerns the left side of the balance sheet." (2) "How can the firm raise cash for required capital expenditures? This question concerns the right side of the balance sheet. The answer to this question involves the firm's capital structure which represents the proportions of the firm's financing from current and long-term debt and equity." (3) "How should short term operating cash flows be managed? This question concerns the upper portion of the balance sheet." In my experience I have found that in most people's personal lives a great amount of thought goes into what assets we should invest, some thought to managing short-term operating cash flows, and the least amount of thought to the individual's (or individual family's) capital structure.

7. Ross, Westerfield, and Jaffe, *Corporate Finance* and John Graham and Campbell Harvey, "The Theory and Practice of Corporate Finance," *Journal of Financial Economics*, May/June 2011.

8. www.nytimes.com/2011/08/03/business/aaa-rating-is-a-rarity-in-business.html?pagewanted=all&_r=0. This potentially excludes some big insurers and some government-affiliated organizations. Arguably all large companies have different forms of short-term debt such as accounts payable, accrued payroll, and so on, and all have lines of credit to facilitate short-term differences in

payables and receivables. The number of AAA companies will, of course, change over time. The concept, which is a key driver, is expressed well in this article: http://blogs.hbr.org/financial-intelligence/2009/07/when-is-debt-good.html. See also Ross, Westerfield, and Jaffe, *Corporate Finance*, 548, and http://usatoday30.usatoday.com/money/companies/management/2005-03-15-aaa-usat_x.htm.

9. See the following for a specific example of a company using debt to buy back shares: www.reuters.com/article/2013/04/24/apple-debt-idUSL2N0D B1X020130424.

10. Eugene F. Brigham and Joel F. Houston, *Fundamentals of Financial Management*, Concise 4th (Mason: Thomson/South-Western, 2004), 465.

    The optimal capital structure is debated and changes throughout time. It is discussed in the following papers: A. Kraus and R. H. Litzenberger, "A State-Preference Model of Optimal Financial Leverage," *Journal of Finance*, September 1973, 911–922; Murray Z. Frank and Vidhan K. Goyal, "Trade-Off and Pecking Order Theories of Debt," February 22, 2005. Available at SSRN: http://ssrn.com/abstract=670543; M. H. Miller. "Debt and Taxes," *Journal of Finance*, 1977, http://ideas.repec.org/a/bla/jfinan/v32y1977i2p261-75.html; S. C. Myers, "The Capital Structure Puzzle," *Journal of Finance* 39, no. 3, Papers and Proceedings, Forty-Second Annual Meeting, American Finance Association, July 1984, 575–592; Working Paper by the Brattle Group, "The Effect of Debt on the Cost of Equity in a Regulatory Setting," Edison Electric Institute (EEI), Washington DC, 2005, http://wpui.wisc.edu/docs/effect_of_debt.pdf; E. Fama and K. French, "Testing Tradeoff and Pecking Order Predictions about Dividends and Debt," *Review of Financial Studies* 15 (Spring 2002): 1–37; www.nber.org/papers/w8782.pdf. Additional details can be found in later chapters and citations.

11. Implicit in this CFO comment are the concepts of Weighted Average Cost of Capital and the Modiglini-Miller Theorem: F. Modigliani and M. Miller, "The Cost of Capital, Corporation Finance and the Theory of Investment," *American Economic Review* 48, no. 3 (1958): 261–297; F. Modigliani and M. Miller, "Corporate Income Taxes and the Cost of Capital: A Correction," *American Economic Review* 53, no. 3 (1963): 433–443; Ross, Westerfield, and Jaffe, *Corporate Finance*, 494–525, addresses this subject in detail. Excerpts from the text follow:

    Page 496: "Managers should choose the capital structure that they believe will have the highest firm value because this capital structure will be most beneficial to the firm's stockholders."

    Page 499: "Modigliani and Miller (MM or M&M) have a convincing argument that a firm cannot change the total value of its outstanding securities before changing the proportions of its capital structure. In other words, the value of a firm is always the same under different capital structures. In still other words, no capital structure is any better or worse than any other capital structure for the firm's stockholders. This rather pessimistic result is the famous MM Proposition 1."

Page 500: "MM Proposition 1 (no taxes): The value of the levered firm is the same as the value of the unlevered firm. This is one of the most important results in all of corporate finance. In fact, it is generally considered the beginning point of modern managerial finance."

Page 510: "In the presence of corporate taxes, the firm's value is positively related to its debt."

Page 511: "Value is maximized for the capital structure paying the least in taxes. In other words, the manager should choose the capital structure that the IRS hates the most. We will show that due to a quirk in U.S. tax law, the proportions of the pie allocated to taxes is less for the levered firm than it is for the unlevered firm. Thus managers should select high leverage."

Chapter 17, Page 526: "Capital Structure Limits to the Use of Debt": "Should managers really set their firm's debt to value ratios near 100 percent? If so, why do real world companies have, as we show later in this chapter, rather modest levels of debt?"

Page 536: Integration of Tax Effects and Financial Distress Costs. "The tax shield increases the value of the levered firm. Financial distress costs lower the value of the levered firm. The two offsetting factors produce an optimal amount of debt. According to the static theory, the R(WACC) falls initially because of the tax advantage of debt. Beyond point B★, it begins to rise because of financial distress costs."

Page 537: "Our discussion implies that a firm's capital structure decision involves a tradeoff between the tax benefits of debt and the costs of financial distress. In fact, this approach . . ."

Also see the following sections: 17.1, "Costs of Financial Distress," page 526; 17.2, "Description of Financial Distress Costs," page 528; and "Indirect Costs of Financial Distress," page 530.

12. The notion of constant debt ratios over time for corporations, and therefore an increase of their outstanding debt over time (and my subsequent investigation of this phenomena), was triggered by a lecture that Joel Stern gave at the University of Chicago in the Fall of 2012.

13. Ross, Westerfield, and Jaffe, *Corporate Finance*, Chapter 15. This is true with respect to corporate bonds. There are examples of certain asset-backed securities such as equipment trust certificates that railroads have used (among others) that either have direct amortization or a toggle feature that can trigger amortization. There also are mortgage-backed securities that contain an

income stream that is comprised of both principal and interest payments. Many private company bank loans are subject to amortization terms. The fact that these loans and securities exist does not preclude the fact that publicly traded corporate debt is issued on an interest-only basis.

While no publicly traded companies issue bonds with built-in amortization, there are indeed amortizing bonds issued in the private equity markets. Also, corporations will establish sinking funds for their bonds where the money needed to repay the principal is put into escrow. However, the company still controls the cash, and the ongoing payments it makes on its debt will be interest only, that is, the only time you will receive a repayment of the principal is when the bond is called or matures. An individual can, of course, create a sinking fund as well.

14. Ziv Bodie, Alex Kane, and Alan Marcus, *Investments*, 9th ed. (New York: McGraw-Hill, 2011), Section 12.1, "The Behavioral Critique in Investments." Implicit in this section are the ideas of behavior finance. Investors may accept the financial theory outlined in these ideas but be unwilling to implement them. This can occur due to a number of reasons. The discussion in this section of the text is largely based on Nicholas Barberis and Richard Thaler, "A Survey of Behavioral Finance," in *Handbook of the Economics of Finance*, ed. G. M. Constantinides, M. Harris, and R. Stulz, 1053–1128 (Amsterdam: Elsevier, 2003).

Page 385: "Prospect Theory modifies the analytic description of rational risk-averse investors found in standard financial theory" from Bodie, Kane, and Marcus.

Prospect Theory originated with a highly influential paper about decision making under uncertainty by D. Kahneman and A. Tversky, "Prospect Theory. An Analysis of Decision under Risk," *Econometrica* 47 (1979): 263–291. The ideas in this theory and in behavioral finance are important to understand and overlap with the ideas in the book. Combining behavioral finance with traditional finance can help an advisor gain a better understanding of individuals' feelings toward debt, their risk reward objectives, and their optimal debt ratios.

15. The information in this chapter is to be considered in a holistic way as a part of the book and not to be considered on a stand-alone basis. This includes, but is not limited to, the discussion of risks of each of these ideas as well as all of the disclaimers throughout the book. The material is presented with a goal of encouraging thoughtful conversation and rigorous debate on the risks and potential benefits of the concepts between you and your advisors based on your unique situation, risk tolerance, and goals.

Chapter 2

The Basic Idea: Limiting the Costs, the Impacts, and the Duration of Financial Distress

L et us, now turn to the basic idea—the key theoretical and practical underpinning—of this book. It all begins with the notions of *financial distress* and the *costs of financial distress*, which are frequently turned to concepts when discussing the fortunes of companies.[1] In this chapter these concepts—along with others that flow out of them—will be applied to individuals and families. We will then point out the many potential benefits of taking a more balanced approach to debt and of relying on one's Indebted Strengths—Increased Liquidity, Flexibility, Leverage, and Survivability—to lessen the potential costs, impacts, and duration of financial distress.

For a company, then, according to *Corporate Finance* (Ross, Westerfield, and Jaffe 2013),

> Financial distress is a term that defines the events preceding and including bankruptcy such as a violation of loan contracts. Financial distress is comprised of the legal and administrative costs of liquidation or reorganization (direct costs); and an impaired ability to do business and an incentive toward selfish strategies such as taking large risks, under-investing, and milking a property (indirect costs).

Throughout this book, financial distress, when applied to individuals and families, will mean much the same thing. That is, an individual or family will be said to be in financial distress when the individual or family has trouble honoring financial commitments and paying bills, a situation that, if unrelieved, can lead to bankruptcy. Similarly, the costs of financial distress—which we'll shortly look at in more detail as comprising both *direct* and *indirect* costs—are those associated with being in financial distress. We'll also expand this basic lexicon to look at the duration of financial distress, as well as the impact it has on the person or family experiencing it.

Risk of Financial Distress

With the definition of financial distress behind us, let's now turn to the associated concept of *risk of financial distress*, that is, how likely are you or your family to actually enter into a state of financial distress? Factors to be considered in assessing how likely you are to be put into financial distress include the following:

- Are you a single or dual income household?
- How stable or volatile is your income stream or streams?
- How likely is it that you (or your spouse) will lose your job for any reason?
- If you (or your spouse) lose your job, how long would it take to replace that income?
- If there is a national severe recession or depression or other financial crisis, how likely is it to directly impact your job(s) and income stream(s)?

- If there is a severe recession or depression or other financial crisis, what will its likely impact be on you and your family?
- How much wealth—how big a cushion—do you ultimately have in reserve?
- How likely are you to be affected by uninsurable or noninsured natural disasters?
- Are there others relying on you and your income—children, parents, and so on—who might suddenly have extreme financial needs that you would feel morally or ethically compelled to assist with?

Unfortunately, there is little you can do to directly change your risk of financial distress, other than perhaps preparing for an alternative career or job—and a place to live and a way to be healthy and happy—if you lose your current position, your income stream falters, or your costs go up dramatically.

> While financial distress itself cannot easily or usually be directly moderated, the likely impact, costs, and duration of financial distress *can* in many cases be addressed with the ideas and practices found in this book.

The Direct and Indirect Costs of Financial Distress

As Figure 2.1 shows, as used in this book and when applied to individuals and families, there are two types of costs of financial distress. The first are the *direct costs of financial distress*, which include fees, penalties, and other monetary costs of being in financial distress. Examples might include penalties assessed on late credit card payments and the higher interest rates that are triggered, amounts used to consult with an attorney or accountant, the increased cost of getting a loan if you have questionable credit, and in the worst case, bankruptcy costs. Perhaps the biggest potential risk of all, however, is the possibility of losing one's assets, including a home foreclosure or the repossession or forced liquidation of physical or financial assets.

On the other hand, while the *indirect costs of financial distress* are not monetary in nature, they do include all of the other ways that financial distress can affect you or your family. For a company, indirect costs

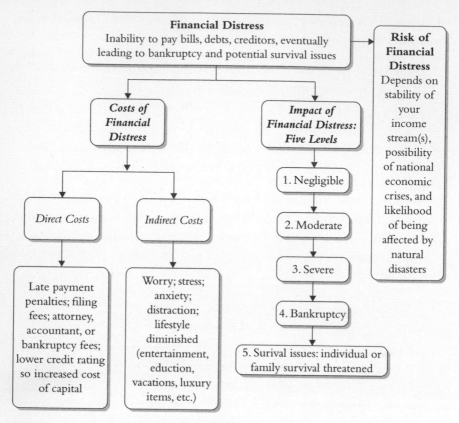

Figure 2.1 Financial Distress Flowchart
Tom Anderson © 2013.

include the loss of customers and suppliers, the loss of morale and focus, the inability to retain key employees, the rapid exodus of irreplaceable management personnel, and ultimately the very viability of the company's core business model. For an individual or family, then, the indirect costs start with worry, stress, anxiety, and distraction, and can lead to an overall diminishment of lifestyle and enjoyment, as well as a ratcheting back on essentials like education and health care, not to mention a reduction in vacations, spending on luxury items, and so on.

The Impact of Financial Distress: Five Levels

In addition to the costs of financial distress, another key factor is the *impact* of financial distress, that is, how bad is the financial distress and its resultant impacts in terms of direct and indirect costs? I have broken down the impact of financial distress into the following five levels:

1. When financial distress is incipient but hasn't really taken hold, there is Level 1 or negligible impacts.
2. Then, as things get worse, there are the moderate impacts of Level 2.
3. Then, at Level 3, severe impacts are experienced.
4. Level 4 brings us to bankruptcy.
5. Finally, beyond bankruptcy, if things get even worse, survival issues arise at Level 5. Here, physical health, an individual's or family's living situation, and even death—for example, from an inability to pay for food, shelter, medicine, and medical care—become real possibilities.

The Duration of Financial Distress

The last major factor to consider is *the duration of financial distress*. While every individual and family will experience financial distress in a unique way dependent on the exact circumstances at hand, there are a number of general statements that can be made about the duration of financial distress:

- First, obviously, the longer the duration of the financial distress, the worse it is for everyone involved.
- Second, indirect costs—worry and anxiety, for example—will take an accelerating toll over time, regardless of the level of financial distress.
- Third, the direct costs of financial distress will accumulate over time, another reason why it is critical to find ways of limiting the duration of financial distress.
- Fourth and finally, the higher the level of financial distress, the more important it is to limit its duration; that is, an individual or family can remain in negligible or even moderate financial distress for quite a while and remain functional, but severe financial distress, bankruptcy, and the survival stage can only be sustained for a relatively short period of time without disastrous consequences.

It was stated earlier that other than making a frank assessment of your *risk of financial distress*, there isn't much you can do to directly change the likelihood that you will eventually experience some degree of financial distress. However, if you already have some wealth there is some very good news: *Both the costs, indirect and direct, as well as the impact level and duration of financial distress, may be able to be greatly moderated or even prevented by making use of the Strategic Debt Philosophy and Practices described in this book.*

The Four Indebted Strengths: A First Look

This brings us to the four key qualities or Indebted Strengths that flow from the strategic use of debt:

1. *Increased Liquidity*—having more ready access to liquid funds or cash.
2. *Increased Flexibility*—having more options for addressing the direct and indirect costs of financial distress and for moderating the level of impact.
3. *Increased Leverage*—in good times, you have the ability to enhance and accelerate the accumulation of wealth.
4. *Increased Survivability*—a diminished likelihood that real survival issues, to your way of life or to life itself, will arise.

The bottom line is that the costs (direct and indirect), the level of impact, and the duration of financial distress can all be diminished by becoming aware of and taking advantage of your Indebted Strengths, as the flowchart in Figure 2.2 shows.

The One Thing You Must Consider!

To help bring these ideas home and make them more concrete, let's consider an example, which also just happens to be the one thing you should consider doing once you have been exposed to the ideas in this book. As Chapter 4 will discuss in detail, if you have at least several hundred thousand dollars in after-tax funds invested in a diversified

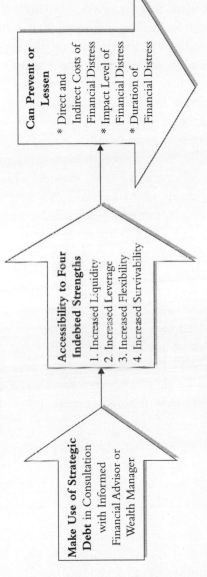

How the Power of Debt Gives You Accessibility to Your Indebted Strengths and Can Prevent or Lessen the Elements of Financial Distress

Make Use of Strategic Debt in Consultation with Informed Financial Advisor or Wealth Manager

Accessibility to Four Indebted Strengths
1. Increased Liquidity
2. Increased Leverage
3. Increased Flexibility
4. Increased Survivability

Can Prevent or Lessen
* Direct and Indirect Costs of Financial Distress
* Impact Level of Financial Distress
* Duration of Financial Distress

Figure 2.2 Power of Debt Flowchart
Tom Anderson © 2013.

portfolio, you are probably eligible for a portfolio-based or assets-based loan facility—an ABLF—to be put into place.

Generally, you will be able to borrow—at reasonable rates—a percentage of these assets. For discussion purposes this will likely be about half of the investments that you pledge in order to get this loan facility. This can vary widely (higher or lower) depending on the assets you have pledged and the firm that is lending the money. See Appendix C for more discussion on advance rates and eligibility.

Generally, the greater the amount you have invested and pledged, the better the interest rate you'll get, and typically the rate you can get on an ABLF will be among the lowest cost source of funds available to you. While getting a good or great rate is often possible, as the case studies will illustrate, what is even more important is the flexibility and cushion it can provide you in a wide variety of circumstances.

What's good about an ABLF? You can access the money quickly, it costs you nothing to put into place, no interest is charged until you actually make use of some portion of the money, and you are not required to make any specific monthly payment.[2]

Now, if you have a line of credit in place and a natural disaster strikes, or if you lose your job, or if an emergency operation that is not covered by insurance arises, guess what? You will have a substantial, immediate, liquid cushion that increases your flexibility generally and lets you address whatever real-time needs have arisen. If this disaster would have otherwise put you into a long period of financial distress, that duration will be shortened, and there's a good chance the ABLF will keep you at or below the moderate financial stress impact level.

> If you do nothing else that this book suggests, please, please, talk to your advisors, determine if you qualify, and evaluate the risks and benefits of having an ABLF in place for you!

Again, there are no costs and limited reasons not to have this cushion available to you if and when you need it. Loan terms can, of course, vary by institution and change over time. Review the documentation from your particular firm and have your advisor discuss any risks or disadvantages for your particular situation.

The thing about your Indebted Strengths—the ability to take advantage of Increased Liquidity, Flexibility, Leverage, and Survivability—is that they are *inherently already yours*. Just by dint of having accumulated a reasonable amount of wealth, there is a way to proactively protect yourself and your family if and when financial distress, or disaster of any kind, comes your way.

Chapter 2: Summary and Checklist

This chapter reviewed the basic idea—the basic theoretical model—at the heart of Strategic Debt Philosophy. The model revolves around a debt philosophy that understands the costs (direct and indirect), impact level (five levels), and duration of financial distress, a concept that is usually only applied to companies. It then described how your Indebted Strengths—Increased Liquidity, Flexibility, Leverage, and Survivability—can lessen or reduce the various elements of financial distress should you or your family be subjected to it at some point. It then gave the example of putting a line of credit into place and urged you to consider doing this now, as something that may greatly help you in case an emergency or disaster, financial or otherwise, comes your way.[3]

Checklist

- ❏ Do the concepts of financial distress, the direct and indirect costs of financial distress, the impact level of financial distress, and the duration of financial distress all make sense to you?
- ❏ Are you now aware that while you cannot usually do much to change the risk that you or your family will one day encounter serious financial distress, the ideas in this book can help to lessen the impact level, the costs (direct and indirect), and the duration of that financial distress?
- ❏ Does the concept of *Indebted Strengths*—the Increased Liquidity, Flexibility, Leverage, and Survivability that comes to you from making intelligent use of strategic debt—make sense to you?

❑ Do you understand that virtually everyone who qualifies should consider having an ABLF in place?

❑ Do you already have an ABLF in place, and if not, are you committed to putting one in place as soon as possible?

Notes

1. Stephen A. Ross, Randolph Westerfield, and Jeffrey Jaffe, *Corporate Finance*, 10th ed. (New York: McGraw-Hill, 2013), 526–534. The material in the textbook refers to the ideas expressed in the following papers and the ideas in this section therefore indirectly do as well: "The High Cost of Going Bankrupt," *Los Angeles Times*, Orange County Edition, December 6, 1995. Taken from Lexis/Nexis; M. J. White, "Bankruptcy Costs and the New Bankruptcy Code," *Journal of Finance*, May 1983, 455–488; E. I. Altman, "A Further Empirical Investigation of the Bankruptcy Cost Questions," *Journal of Finance*, September 1984, 1067–1089; Lawrence A. Weiss, "Bankruptcy Resolution: Direct Costs and Violation of Priority Claims," *Journal of Financial Economics* 27 (1990), 285–314; J. B. Warner, "Bankruptcy Costs: Some Evidence," *Journal of Finance*, May 1997, 337–347; Stephen J. Lubben, "The Direct Costs of Corporate Reorganization: An Empirical Examination of Professional Fees in Chapter 11 Cases," *American Bankruptcy Law Journal*, 2000, 509–522; Auturo Bris, Ivo Welch, and Ning Zhu, "The Costs of Bankruptcy: Chapter 7 Liquidation versus Chapter 11 Reorganization," *Journal of Finance*, June 2006, 1253–1303; Gregor Andrade and Steven N. Kaplan, "How Costly Is Financial (Not Economic) Distress? Evidence from Highly Leveraged Transactions That Became Distressed," *Journal of Finance*, October 1998, 1443–1493; Yuval Bar-Or, "An Investigation of Expected Distress Costs" (unpublished paper, Wharton School, University of Pennsylvania, March 2000); David M. Cutler and Lawrence H. Summers, "The Costs of Conflict Resolution and Financial Distress: Evidence from the Texaco—Penzoil Litigation," *Rand Journal of Economics*, Summer 1988, 157–172.

2. ABLFs can be either what are called purpose or nonpurpose loans. A *nonpurpose loan* is a line of credit or loan that is based on the eligible securities held in a brokerage account. They can be used for any suitable purpose except to purchase, trade, or carry securities or repay debt that was used to purchase, trade, or carry securities, and should not be deposited into a brokerage account. A *purpose loan*, or margin loan offered by a brokerage firm, is a revolving line of credit based on securities held in a brokerage account. These loans are primarily used to purchase securities but can be used for any other purpose. The text is not intended to imply that having an ABLF is guaranteed liquidity. It is important to note that many ABLFs are not committed

facilities. Therefore, a lender has no obligation to make an advance and can reject any advance request from a borrower in its sole discretion. Although ABLFs can minimize the risk of distress, they could in fact actually increase your risk of distress. If you have an ABLF and the market drops (including the securities securing your loan), you could be forced into a margin call with no additional securities/collateral to deposit and in a situation where you don't have liquid funds to pay down the loan. Accordingly, you could be forced to sell the securities collateral at that time, which if the market is depressed, would be at a bad price and potentially trigger tax consequences. We will look at ways to reduce this risk later in the book, but it is essential to recognize that the risk exists. There are other risks as well, including that many ABLFs are demand facilities, which means that they can demand repayment at any time. Also, the lender usually maintains the right to liquidate the securities held collateral at any time. You must work with your advisors to understand and mitigate these risks. All examples within the book will assume that credit is available, securities are eligible and that the lender is willing to continue advancing money.

3. The information in this chapter is to be considered in a holistic way as a part of the book and not to be considered on a stand-alone basis. This includes, but is not limited to, the discussion of risks of each of these ideas as well as all of the disclaimers throughout the book. The material is presented with a goal of encouraging thoughtful conversation and rigorous debate on the risks and potential benefits of the concepts between you and your advisors based on your unique situation, risk tolerance, and goals.

Chapter 3

Strategic Debt Practices: An Overview

C hapter 2 provided an overview of Strategic Debt *Philosophy*—the ideas and theoretical underpinnings behind the use of Strategic Debt. In this chapter I will turn more directly to Strategic Debt *Practices* and applications—to real-world techniques and action steps—and the likely advantages and results of applying the philosophical stance and theoretical ideas we've been considering. The major Strategic Debt Practices that will be touched on include

- Understanding and taking advantage of your Indebted Strengths
- Achieving and maintaining an ideal debt ratio
- How to calculate your own current debt ratio
- When to pay down your debt, and when not to
- A quick first look at a number of advanced practices to be covered in Part III

Understanding and Taking Advantage of Strategic Debt Philosophy

Earlier I provided a brief definition of the four Indebted Strengths of Increased Liquidity, Flexibility, Leverage, and Survivability. Given the importance of these four concepts both as philosophical ideas and as real-world practices that can make a tremendous difference in your life, let's return to and expand on each of them with a simple example in mind. By understanding exactly how the four strengths apply in a real-world situation, you will likely be more able to see how they might be applicable in your own case as well, leading you to more readily embrace the wider variety of Strategic Debt Practices.

The Smith family consists of Mr. Carl Smith; Mrs. Lesley Smith; Cole, their 17-year-old son; and Lauren, their 14-year-old daughter. The Smith family's primary residence is in a gorgeous rural area and has been in the family for generations. As a result it is owned free and clear, and the Smiths also have liquid assets of $3 million that are eligible to be pledged. After discussing the ideas in this book, the Smith family has put into place an ABLF enabling them to borrow up to $1.5 million dollars at a low interest rate, with no amortization or required payment schedule. Assuming funds are available, the Smiths can access these funds either by wiring money or by writing regular checks out of a checkbook they've been provided.[1]

A month later a major hurricane strikes, causing the creek behind the Smiths' home to flood their basement and cause substantial damage to the first floor of their now mostly uninhabitable home. Fortunately, it can all be fixed, but (a) it will take several hundred thousand dollars, and (b) in the meantime the Smiths have first moved to a nearby hotel, and then into a rental home on a three-month lease. Also, fortunately, the Smiths have flood insurance, but they are well aware that the insurance won't cover everything and that it will take months to work through the paperwork and get fully reimbursed for the damage that was covered by their policy.

There's one final "fortunately" in this story: Fortunately, the Smiths have *already* put an ABLF into place and can start writing necessary checks immediately at an interest rate that is not too onerous. That is, their ABLF immediately gives them *Increased Liquidity. With the checkbook they already have in their hands*, they are able to put down money to start the necessary repairs and get into their temporary housing. There is nothing like having ready access to liquid cash when you need it, and the Smiths are very appreciative of their ABLF checkbook.

The ABLF also gives the Smiths *Increased Flexibility*—for handling their financial affairs and investments the way they want to. Instead of being forced to sell off any of their current investments at a disadvantageous point in time, they have the flexibility to cover the expenses now and decide when they want to raise funds. Further, as time goes on they will have a better understanding of exactly how much insurance is covering and how much they will need from their account.

Moreover, as soon as the Smiths realize that they can easily take care of their new financial burden with their line of credit, all of the potential indirect costs—including worry, stress, anxiety, and distraction—simply vanish.

Ultimately, it is estimated that the repairs will cost about $100,000 more than insurance will cover. Since the stock market has recently sold off dramatically, their financial advisor feels that now would be an inappropriate time to liquidate any of their holdings. Their advisor feels that in the long run the Smiths will be able to continue to make more on their portfolio than it costs them to borrow money to pay for their immediate needs. Here, then, the Smiths are taking advantage of the *Increased Leverage* that comes with being able to borrow money at a relatively low interest rate to pay for their immediate needs.

WITH AN ABLF *YOU* BECOME THE DECISION MAKER!

I cannot overstate the importance of the ability to stay invested during a disaster or difficult times. With a properly structured line of credit proactively in place with availability, *you* are in control. You can determine when you want to sell assets to raise cash.[2]

Liquidity / Flexibility / Leverage / Survivability

Perhaps most importantly, in addition to the Increased Liquidity, Flexibility, and Leverage that has come to them through their use of their ABLF, the Smiths also have *Increased Survivability* in their back pocket. With the help of their ABLF checkbook, they are able to move to a hotel and then find a rental home, buy new clothing and possessions, and have their children continue in their respective schools, all without missing a beat—despite the immediate outlay of tens and ultimately hundreds of thousands of dollars that became necessary.

That is, the Smiths' basic way of life was able to continue and their overall standard of living remained the same, despite falling prey to a

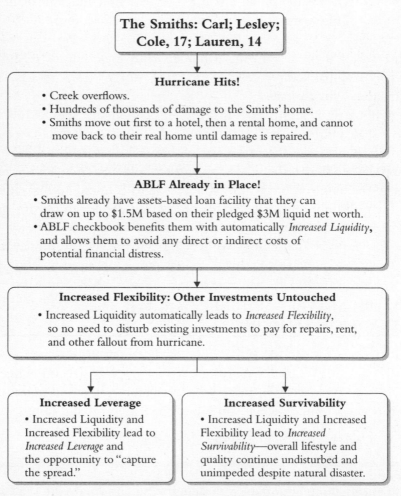

Figure 3.1 The Smiths' Flowchart: An Example of the Use of Indebted Strengths
Tom Anderson © 2013.

disaster that took them by surprise. Within a few months' time, despite all that has occurred, all is well again. Figure 3.1 presents a visual summary of how the Smiths were able to use each of the four Indebted Strengths to their advantage.

Achieving and Maintaining an Optimal Debt-to-Asset Ratio

The fourth tenet of Strategic Debt Philosophy—as described in Chapter 2—is to "Set Your Sights on an Optimal Personal Debt Ratio." In a world where we are constantly told that all personal debt is bad and should be eliminated as soon as possible, the mere recognition that such a thing as an optimal debt ratio exists constitutes a bold and out-of-the-box thought. The next step—to assess and determine one's current debt ratio and then over time find ways of optimizing it   should be a lifelong practice. That is, moving oneself or one's family to an ideal debt ratio is a multistep and probably multiyear process, starting with the recognition that not all debt is bad, then moving on to the notion that some debt—especially the right kind of debt—can be quite good.

Naturally, the ideal debt-to-asset ratio—a ratio that is obtained by dividing your total debt by your total assets—is going to differ for you or your family depending on your circumstances, your age, your retirement goals, and so on. Unfortunately, however, because of the rampant antidebt paradigm that holds so much sway over so many, very few individuals or families even begin to ask the following kinds of questions:

- What is your optimal debt ratio?
- What do you need to do to achieve an optimal debt ratio?
- How is this optimal debt ratio likely to change over time? What will your optimal debt ratio be in
  - One year?
  - Three years?
  - Five years?
  - Ten years?
  - During retirement?
  - Upon death?

- How should your debt be structured?
  - How much should be fixed?
  - How much should be floating?
  - How much should be amortized?

Put differently, the vast majority of individuals, including wealthy individuals and families, find it hard to think outside the box and consider the possibilities being discussed here. It's no surprise, therefore, that they ask no questions relevant to these possibilities, do no hard thinking about them, and certainly take no proactive action with respect to achieving an optimal debt ratio with correctly structured debt.

This brings us, of course, to the question of *what percentage, exactly, represents an ideal debt ratio*? To answer this, let's start with a quick return to the world of companies. Research shows that most companies have debt ratios—total debt divided by total assets—in the neighborhood of around 40 to 50 percent, although it tends to vary by industry. In some industries, the average is around 60 percent, and in others it tends to hover closer to 30 percent. At the outer bounds, although there are exceptions, there are few companies that have a debt ratio of more than 80 percent, and few that have debt ratios of less than 20 percent.[3]

What, then, about individuals? By applying many of the same principles of corporate finance but ratcheting them down to be more conservative for the individual, *the optimal debt ratio for a wealthy individual or family can be defined as being around 25 percent and will generally range between 15 and 35 percent*, based on circumstances, including the individual's or family's risk of financial distress and the likely costs (direct and indirect), impact level, and duration of potential financial distress.

Unfortunately, what normally tends to happen is that people either have much higher debt ratio (which is oftentimes structured in completely the wrong way), or they tend to have a debt ratio that is much lower than this and therefore suboptimal. So if your ratio is 45 percent or above, you are taking on considerable risk, but if your ratio is 10 percent or less, that, too, indicates a situation that is likely far from optimal.

Another problematic tendency is for individuals and families to have their debt ratios vary widely over time. We will look at times when paying down debt can make sense, but our goal as we move through

HOW DO YOU DETERMINE OPTIMAL?

Looking forward, nobody truly knows what the optimal capital structure or balance sheet design is for any particular company. Only history can judge that. Similarly, I would suggest that nobody knows the optimal ratio for a particular individual or family. The purpose of this book is not to focus on a specific number or precise capital structure, but rather to challenge you to work with your advisors to determine your optimal debt ratio range based on your own individual circumstances.

My work has shown that 15–35 percent is optimal. I narrow in on the 25 percent target and adjust it up and down based on a family's risk of financial distress and the likely costs (direct and indirect), impact level, and duration of their potential financial distress as well as their suitability, risk tolerance, and overall objectives.

Now, some who read this material may feel that this is too aggressive and would shave 10 percent off of the range (perhaps 5–25 percent, with 15 percent as optimal). Others may feel that my range is too conservative (that it should be higher, like 25–45 percent), and still others may feel that it is too narrow (that the range should be wider, such as 20–60 percent) or that it should evolve within a wider range over time (for example, perhaps your optimal debt ratio is also a function of age).

By engaging in these considerations, you are on the right path. To those who are outside of my ranges, I encourage free-flowing debate and conversation, and would briefly make the following observations:

To those who feel the range should be lower: Are you truly benefiting from the Increased Leverage that would otherwise be available to you?

To those who feel it should be higher: Please read Appendix C and make sure you are prepared for a future that could be dramatically different from your past. You are likely increasing your reliance on your income being at least the same looking forward. A base case that you should stress-test is an extended period where

(Continued)

HOW DO YOU DETERMINE OPTIMAL? (*Continued*)

you are unemployed, interest rates are rising (potentially increasing the cost of your debt and pushing down the value of your bonds), housing prices are falling, and equity prices are falling as well—a quadruple threat.

To those who suggest it evolves over time: Perhaps, indeed, the range should be a little higher earlier in life, with the range suggested here being appropriate for later in life. In my mind there is some truth to this, particularly for those who are in the accumulation phase, because it addresses the income component and not just the asset aspect of the formula. Companies do look at debt-to-income ratios as well in their determination of the optimal structure, and I do address this idea briefly in Appendix B. However, early in life your risk and cost of distress tends to be high, which argues for a lower debt ratio.

On average, I find that too often debt ratios start out way higher than my suggested range and then blow right through it on a path to zero. By virtue of this process, I also typically find that people lack the flexibility that having more liquid, after-tax investment funds would provide them.

As a friendly reminder, this book is geared toward people who already have sufficient assets and want to position their life so that they can retire in relative comfort. *With respect to this demographic, my research shows—and the case studies will illustrate—that 15 to 35 percent, with a target of 25 percent, is the optimal starting place for conversations and discussion.*

the book will be to challenge this high-to-low/zero approach. If you remember back to the second tenet of Strategic Debt Philosophy discussed in Chapter 1, another hallmark of companies is that they tend to have fairly constant debt ratios over time. While it may make sense to raise or lower your debt ratio over time depending on the stage of life you are in, if you are experiencing wild swings in your debt ratio, there may be a problem in the handling of your financial affairs.

Remember the crucial point—when reviewing the case studies in the later chapters—that corporate debt ratios remain *relatively constant over time.*[4]

The next section will discuss how to examine your balance sheet to determine your current debt ratio. The key point for now is to understand that there is indeed such a thing as an optimal debt ratio for wealthy individuals and families, and that if you don't yet understand how Strategic Debt Philosophy can benefit you, then you are unlikely to ever attain this ideal ratio. You could be taking too much or too little risk. Conversely, setting your sights on achieving that ideal ratio makes it far more likely that you will achieve it.

Calculating Your Debt-to-Asset Ratio

The formula used to calculate your debt ratio is easy to state:

debt-to-asset ratio = total debt/total assets

Thus, your debt ratio is the ratio of your total debt to your total assets and is typically expressed as a percentage. If your total debt is $1 million dollars and your total assets are worth $4 million dollars, then your debt ratio is $1 million divided by $4 million, or 25 percent.[5]

In order to accurately calculate the ratio you need to accurately account for *total debt* and *total assets*, which will involve some paperwork and some legwork in order to get current and accurate totals for both categories. It may be helpful to work closely with your accountant and your financial advisor or private banker when going through these calculations.

Tables 3.1 and 3.2 will give you some general guidelines as to what to include and what not to include under both the Total Debt and Total Assets categories. Since I believe that you are better off being conservative in these calculations—underestimating your debt ratio is potentially a much bigger problem than overestimating it—you should probably reflect the value of all your debts at or near their likely

Table 3.1   Total Debt

You are better served by being conservative and overstating the value of your liabilities.

Include	Potentially Exclude
• Face value of all mortgages, loans, debts • Cash needs over next 24 months • Tax obligations due next 24 months • Present value of future tax obligations that you feel should be included • Present value of all contractual obligations that cannot be broken (lease payments, long-term rentals) • Anything else you think should be included	• Tax obligations on tax deferred plans and tax obligations where you can control the timing of the taxable event (401K, deferred compensation plans)[6]

Table 3.2   Total Assets

You are better served by being conservative and understating your assets in the formula.

Include	Potentially Exclude
• Market value of all publicly held securities, cash, and investments across all account structures (taxable, tax deferred)	• All personal property valued under $5K ("stuff")
• Partnerships/Closely Held Business valued at a 15% discount to comparable publicly traded companies plus an additional 20% liquidity discount	• Everything that is not vested (deferred compensation, options)
• Vehicles at 80% of Kelly Blue Book Trade—In Value (liquidity discount)	• Some people exclude the value of their primary residence *(see next section for a detailed discussion of this)*
• Real Estate at a price that could be received in 90 days less a 6% commission	• 529 plans (effectively serve to fund a future liability)
• Art and jewelry, antiques, collectibles (worth more than $5K), valued at price item(s) would receive at auction tomorrow less 10% commission	• Anything else that you think should be excluded

highest possible value and the value of all your assets at or near their lowest possible value. To be extra-conservative, you should also consider including future tax obligations that will become due (such as on the sale of a business, the sale of options, or unrealized capital gains on stocks), as well as the face value of any debt that you have personally guaranteed.

Should Your Primary Residence Be Included in Your Debt Ratio?

The simplest way to approach your primary residence—your main home—is to include its appraised value or its assessed value under the total assets column (although, again, you want to be conservative here), and any mortgage debt or home equity loan or line that has been accessed under your total debts. Keep in mind that given its tax-advantaged status (in today's tax code and up to a limit), mortgage debt, especially at current low interest rates, is among the very best kind of debts that you can have. In this sense, there's every reason to take on debt on your primary residence—as well as on any secondary properties, as discussed in more detail in Chapter 6—as long as you stay within the general desirable debt ratio of between 15 and 35 percent. Along these lines, it generally makes sense to include your primary residence in your overall debt ratio calculations.

On the other hand, it is arguable that your main home—your primary residence—is not something that you want to have debt associated with, and that it should be owned free and clear and thus excluded from your debt ratio. After all, one has to live somewhere, and in this way your primary residence can be seen more as an expense than an asset. Importantly, owning your primary residence outright can decrease the intensity level, the direct and indirect costs, and the duration of financial distress should it come your way. That is, if something goes really wrong, then you don't have to worry about paying your mortgage, and instead your housing expenses would be limited to property taxes and maintenance. In this sense, owning your primary residence outright—if you can afford it—increases your survivability in a direct and palpable way and may enable you to sleep better at night.

AN ADVANCED HYBRID APPROACH TO CONSIDER

Consider excluding the value of your primary residence from your assets in calculating your debt ratio (you have to live somewhere), but still place a mortgage against the property. You would consider this due to the favorable mortgage terms that exist (tax deductibility and fixed or floating rates lower than most alternatives) and the fact that the mortgage is not subject to a margin call. This is mathematically equal to reducing your optimal debt ratio range.

Example:

Imagine you own two assets: a house worth $750,000 and an investment portfolio worth $2 million. Your assets would traditionally be listed as follows:

$750,000 house
+ $2 million portfolio
= $2.75 million of assets for the denominator in the debt ratio

If you had a $500,000 mortgage then your debt ratio would be $500,000/$2.75 million = an 18% debt ratio.

By using the modified approach, then, for the purpose of this formula, you could consider excluding the house from the assets (reflecting that you have to live somewhere or your desire to own your house outright). Your total assets would be listed at $2 million. Applying the same $500,000 liability/$2 million = a 25% debt ratio. By doing this one could argue that in effect you do own your house outright yet are still embracing a strategic debt philosophy.

Table 3.3 summarizes the pros and cons of owning your primary residence free and clear. Keep in mind that there's no right or wrong here; it's what you feel comfortable with and can live with (and live in!). If you already own your house outright and determine you are

Table 3.3 Should You Own Your House Free and Clear?

Yes—You Should Own Your Primary House Outright!	No—It Is Just Another Asset and One of the Best Assets to Leverage
• Your primary home should be owned outright and excluded from your debt ratio.	• Typically, debt against a primary residence offers some of the best—if not the best—loan terms available, with the greatest flexibility to fix the loan or float it at the lowest rates available to individuals.
• One has to live somewhere, and therefore your primary home is an expense, not an asset.	
• Owning your primary house decreases the likely impact level, direct and indirect costs, and duration of financial distress.	• Paying down your primary residence ties up capital in a relatively illiquid asset.
• If you own your main home free and clear, then if something goes wrong, your housing expenses are limited to property taxes and maintenance.	• You could actually lower your risk and costs of financial distress if you had liquid funds of equal value in an investment account.
	• These funds offer much more flexibility, including the ability to liquidate or leverage as needed.
	• There are very significant tax benefits to the first $1 million dollars of residential real estate debt.
	• If you choose to not have a second home—and many people do not—then the best (and occasionally only) way to embrace an optimal debt ratio is by using this asset.

not optimal, you should know that there are considerable risks—and some outright restrictions—on doing a refinancing on your house and investing the proceeds. It can be a bad idea for many reasons. Later we will discuss getting to optimal, but for now the following ideas are building blocks in the optimal puzzle.

When to Pay Down Your Debt, and When Not To

There is a tendency among many well-off individuals and families to go ahead and pay off some or all of their outstanding debt as soon as they possibly can. Given the pervasive antidebt paradigm (as discussed in the third tenet in Chapter 2), this is not surprising. But once you recognize the value of Strategic Debt and the importance of achieving and maintaining an ideal debt ratio, you can quickly understand why it's important to differentiate between the various types of debt and to learn when to, and when not to, pay down outstanding debt.

One factor is the *kind* of debt that is in question. Appendix A comprises a detailed discussion of "The Varieties of Debt" and makes some distinctions about which types of debt are generally more preferable to have and which kinds really should be jettisoned as soon as possible. One of the factors that must be considered is whether the debt in question is tax advantaged, for example, the debt that comes with owning a mortgage on real estate. With respect to all debt, there is a very important principle to keep in mind:

> Your rate of return on paying down debt is exactly equal to your after-tax cost of that debt.

If you have a mortgage at 3 percent and are in the 39 percent federal and 5 percent state tax bracket, your after-tax cost of that debt is $3\% \times (1 - (.39 + .05)) =$ about 1.68%. If you pay down this debt it is the equivalent of receiving a 1.68 percent rate of return.

A simple example might help to clarify this. Suppose you have a home with $100,000 left on the mortgage principal, and out of the blue you get a work bonus that, after taxes, will leave you with an extra $100,000. Well, you might be tempted to say to yourself, "Heck, I'd rather own our home free and clear, so I'll just use that money to pay off all of the mortgage principal." Well, suppose at the end of the day, with a mortgage loan at 4.5 percent, you will be paying about $4,500 ($4,500 = $100,000 \times 4.5\%$) worth of interest on that mortgage over the course of the year.

However, if that interest is deductible and you are at the 33 percent tax bracket, then that $4,500 you are saving by paying off the principal is really only saving you $3,000 a year ($3,000 = $4,500 \times (1 - .33)$).

The next question you have to ask yourself is whether—if you don't spend that $100,000 on paying off the principal—you can capture the spread and make more than $3,000 a year with that $100,000 intelligently invested.

Put differently, given the after-tax cost of that mortgage debt, you will be earning the equivalent of 3 percent on that $100,000 if you pay off the principal. If you feel you can deploy that same capital to earn greater than 3 percent, you probably shouldn't pay down the principal. If you feel it isn't likely that you can earn greater than that 3 percent, then go ahead and pay down the loan.

In some cases, it's quite clear that debt should be paid down as soon as possible, let's say, credit card debt running at double-digit interest rates—12 percent, 15 percent, or higher. In other cases, as with tax-advantaged mortgage debt or debt on a low interest line of credit, you really want to think it through, especially if you have not yet obtained an ideal debt ratio. To help you think through whether or not you should pay down debt if the opportunity arises, Figure 3.2 presents the major factors to consider, including whether the debt is tax advantaged, whether the debt is at a high or low interest rate, and whether you are at or below your ideal debt ratio.

Work closely with your tax advisor to determine your ability to deduct different kinds of debt and for help in determining your net after-tax cost of debt.

Advanced Practices and Scenarios

Part III of this book covers three types of "advanced" Strategic Debt practices, including

1. *Capturing the spread*, or using the leverage that comes from your indebted strengths to essentially make money on money that you borrow. The question here is simple: Are there any investments in the world that, on average, can beat the cost of your after-tax cost of whatever money you are borrowing?
2. *Financing the purchase of expensive items and assets, including vehicles and real estate:* There are often very advantageous ways of relying on

Figure 3.2 Should I Pay Down My Debt as Soon as Possible?
Tom Anderson © 2013.

your Indebted Strengths to purchase items rather than selling assets or borrowing money from external sources to do so.

3. *Generating tax-advantaged income in retirement or divorce*: Very few people know about or take advantage of this, but it is often possible to generate income in a flexible and tax-advantaged manner. There are even ways that, depending on your individual circumstances, you may be able to use an ABLF to access money tax free. In this section we will discuss tax facts with respect to ordinary income, long-term capital gains, and ABLFs.

Chapter 3: Summary and Checklist

This chapter presented an overview of the major Strategic Debt Practices that you should be aware of. The first of these practices is gaining a general and deeper understanding of the four Indebted Strengths—Increased Liquidity, Flexibility, Leverage, and Survivability. With a better knowledge of your Indebted Strengths, you are simply more likely to make appropriate inquiries as to how to take advantage of them and then take appropriate actions that will benefit you and your family. To make things clearer, we used the example of the Smith family to show how these four Indebted Strengths might play out in the real world even when disaster strikes.

The second strategic practice concerns achieving and maintaining an ideal debt ratio. We discussed the kinds of questions an individual or family might want to be asking with regard to determining such an ideal ratio for their own situation, and stated that *the ideal debt ratio for a wealthy individual or family is around 25 percent, and will generally range between 15 and 35 percent.*

The next practice concerns when to pay down debt, and when not to. A flow chart was used to show that in addition to avoiding knee-jerk antidebt reactions, the three main questions that should be asked when determining whether or not to pay down debt are whether the debt is tax advantaged (like mortgage debt), whether the debt is at a high or low interest rate, and whether you are currently above, at, or below your ideal debt ratio.

We then introduced three advanced practices that will be covered in Part III. The first is the idea of *capturing the spread*, which refers to targeting a return on investment that is higher than the cost of the debt that you would take on to make that investment. The second is the practice of *self-financing the purchase of expensive items and assets*, including real estate. For example, using an ABLF you can come up with all the money needed to buy the car at a favorable interest rate that is not amortizable. Finally, we introduced the idea of *tax-efficient income in retirement or divorce*, which I will return to in detail in Chapter 7.

There is one final Strategic Debt Practice, covered in Appendix A, which involves the general importance of becoming familiar with the varieties of debt that exist—all of the different types of loans and ways of taking on debt you as an individual or family will typically be exposed to. Some types of debt are simply better than others, and by setting out that information in one place, you can become familiar with it and be more likely to make better decisions regardless of which Strategic Debt Practice you are considering initiating.[7]

Checklist

❑ Did the review of the four Indebted Strengths make sense to you as the chapter moved from ideas and philosophy to real-world practices and applications?

❑ Does the concept of there being an ideal debt ratio (the totality of your debt divided by the totality of your assets) in the 15 to 35 percent range make sense to you?

❑ Do you understand how to calculate your own debt ratio?

❑ Have you gone ahead and actually calculated your debt ratio?

❑ Do you understand why rushing to pay down all debt whenever you can may be a mistake, and that instead you need to consider what type of debt is in question and whether it makes sense to pay it down given the big picture?

❑ Have you taken a look at Appendix A to become familiar with the varieties of debt and their plusses and minuses?

Notes

1. Case studies are for educational and illustrative purposes only. This case assumes eligible assets and that funds are available on the facility. All client situations are unique, and all loans are subject to eligibility and approval by the lender. A lender may deny an advance on an ABLF, preventing the Smith scenario. Pledging assets reduces and may eliminate their liquidity. A market correction could impact market values and/or security eligibility, which could impact the facility size and/or trigger a margin call and/or forced liquidation of assets. See complete disclosures and risks to using an ABLF in Appendix C.

2. See complete ABLF discussion in Appendix C for examples on when your control and liquidity can be compromised with an ABLF.

3. Stephen A. Ross, Randolph Westerfield, and Jeffrey Jaffe, *Corporate Finance*, 10th ed. (New York: McGraw-Hill, 2013), Chapters 15, 16, and 17. In particular readers should look at the following:

Page 488, Section 15.7: Recent Trends in Capital Structure. Examine Figure 15.3, Book Debt Ratio: Total Debt as a Percentage of the Book Value of Equity for U.S. Nonfarm, Nonfinancial Firms from 1995 to 2010. This range has generally been between 60 and 75 percent.

Page 499, Figure 15.4, Market Debt Ratio: Total Debt as a Percentage of the Market Value of Equity for U.S. Nonfarm, Nonfinancial Firms from 1995 to 2010 shows a range of roughly 40–55 percent.

An in-depth study of corporate debt ratios should also reconcile the above points with data from page 549, Section 17.9, Figure 17.4. According to Joseph P. H. Fan, Sheridan Titman, and Gary Twite, "An International Comparison of Capital Structure and Debt Maturity Choices" (unpublished paper, University of Texas at Austin, September 2010), the median leverage ratio of sample firms in 39 different countries from 1991 to 2006 has ranged from slightly over 50 percent to slightly under 10 percent with a lot of firms in the 20 to 30 percent range.

Page 553: "Debt ratios vary across industries. We present three factors determining the target debt to equity ratio:

1. Taxes: Firms with high taxable income should rely more on debt than firms with low taxable income.

2. Types of assets: Firms with a high percentage of intangible assets such as research and development should have low debt. Firms with primarily tangible assets should have higher debt

3. Uncertainty of operating income: firms with high uncertainty of operating income should rely mostly on equity (have minimal debt)

See also Board of Governors of the Federal Reserve System, "Flow of Funds Accounts of the United States," Federal Reserve Statistical Release, June 9, 2011, www.federalreserve.gov/releases/z1/20110609 and www.federalreserve.gov/releases/z1/20110609/z1r-4.pdf. It is interesting that according to the Federal Reserve, in aggregate, individual debt ratios are relatively close to this range.

See also Ziv Bodie, Alex Kane, and Alan Marcus, *Investments*, 9th ed. (New York: McGraw-Hill, 2011), Section 12.1, The Behavioral Critique in Investments, 461–468.

Table 14.3 from Bodie, Kane, and Marcus, shows that companies had Total debt/Total debt + Equity percent in the following ranges:

Three-Year (2002–2004) Medians

	AAA	AA	A	BBB	BB	B
Total Debt/Total debt + Equity percent	12.4	28.3	37.5	42.5	53.7	75.9

Source: "Corporate Rating Criteria," Standard & Poors, 2006.

Of course, additional criteria are used in bond ratings including but not limited to coverage ratios, leverage ratios, liquidity ratios, profitability ratios, and cash-flow-to-debt ratios.

For those who would like more detail on corporate debt ratios I would suggest that you pull a representative sample across multiple industries of various well-known corporations and study their balance sheets. A key consideration is if you look at debt relative to book value or market value.

4. Ross, Westerfield, and Jaffe, *Corporate Finance*, Chapters 15, 16, and 17. In addition, it is important to note that capital structures of individual firms can vary significantly over time. While most firms use target leverage ratios, a recent paper nevertheless concludes that capital structures of individual firms often vary widely over time. See Harry DeAngelo and Richard Roll, "How Stable Are Corporate Capital Structures?" (unpublished paper, Marshall School of Business, University of Southern California, July 2011).

5. Bodie, Kane, and Marcus, *Investments*, Section 12.1, The Behavioral Critique in Investments, 463 and 643. Companies also calculate coverage ratios, leverage ratios, liquidity ratios, profitability ratios, and cash-flow-to-debt ratios. A truly holistic approach should consider more than just a debt-to-equity ratio.

6. Excluding this liability is debatable, which is why it says "potentially exclude." A conservative approach is always to overstate your liabilities. You could include the present value of the tax obligations but in doing so you would need to determine the appropriate discount rate and make a proper estimate as to your future effective tax rate. In Chapter 7 we will see examples on how income can be distributed from tax deferred plans at a much lower rate (as low as zero). We will also see how you can use an ABLF to create tax-advantaged income. Further, occasionally the use an ABLF can enable you to control the timing of taxable events, pushing them into a more favorable tax environment. I would encourage you to revisit this formula after reading the entire book.

7. The information in this chapter is to be considered in a holistic way as a part of the book and not to be considered on a stand-alone basis. This includes, but is not limited to, the discussion of risks of each of these ideas as well as all of the disclaimers throughout the book. The material is presented with a goal of encouraging thoughtful conversation and rigorous debate on the risks and potential benefits of the concepts between you and your advisors based on your unique situation, risk tolerance, and goals.

Part 2

THE ASSETS-BASED LOAN FACILITY

"It is not in the stars to hold our destiny, but in ourselves."
—*William Shakespeare*, Romeo and Juliet

Chapter 4

The Value of an Assets-Based Loan Facility (ABLF)

Y ou may remember that at the end of Chapter 1 there was a
section called, "The One Thing You Must Consider." That
"one thing," of course, was to set up an ABLF in a timely fashion because there are great advantages to doing so. I will therefore go
through the intricacies of an ABLF, including

- What an ABLF is and how it works
- Why virtually every company has an ABLF or the equivalent of an
  ABLF
- The many advantages of having an ABLF in place
- The criticality of being proactive before disaster strikes
- Surviving storms and natural disasters—when you need money now!

- Family finances: First Bank of Mom and Dad; elder care bridge loans
- Taking advantage of opportunities and distressed sales
- Average ABLF usage
- A win-win-win: benefiting yourself, your advisor, and his or her firm

What an ABLF Is and How It Works

Virtually every major financial firm offers what I have labeled an ABLF, or assets-based loan facility. Each firm will typically brand this type of loan facility under some marketing name. There are also secured personal lines of credit, margin accounts, and what are called custom or tailored loans. In this book I will refer to all of these types of loans and lines of credit as ABLFs. Consistent with loans of nearly every type, each institution has full list of rules, regulations, limitations, and disclaimers that you will need to fully understand by working closely with your financial advisor or private banker.

While the details of each firm's lines of credit differ, the general outlines are the same. As someone with a relationship with the firm, you create a pledge account that consists of securities that are both publicly and openly traded and taxable.[1] The firm then agrees to lend you money, at a favorable rate, against the assets held in the pledge account, as long as you maintain a relationship with the firm. In the event you leave the firm and transfer your account elsewhere, you have to pay off the loan first.

The greater the amount of assets you have in the pledge account, the greater the size of the loan facility that can be put in place. And the greater the size of the loan facility, the more favorable the interest rate that will be charged. A rough approximation of the amount of credit available to you is 50 percent of the amount of assets that are pledged. For example, if you have $1 million of qualifying pledged assets, you can typically get an ABLF for up to $500,000. In most cases, it makes sense to put in place the maximum size facility for which you qualify.

When one is pledging assets against a loan, the lender requires that the value of the portfolio must remain consistently above a certain level. If the underlying assets fall below this threshold, the firm can (and will) issue what is called a margin call. A margin call requires that some of the assets in the portfolio be sold at the firm's discretion in order to pay off some, or all, of the amount that was loaned to you.

Obviously, since you are not in control of what would be sold off in this scenario, it is a situation you want to avoid. So while you want to set up an ABLF for the maximum amount that you qualify for—which gets you the best interest rates—you should avoid using all or even most of the loan capacity available to you except in the case of a serious emergency, a family-related financial need, or an extraordinary economic opportunity such as in the case of a distressed sale. Thus, *it is very important that you monitor the amount that has been loaned to you on the ABLF*, and that you embrace an investment philosophy that minimizes the volatility of the assets that are securing your ABLF. *Volatility* refers to how volatile a security is, or how likely it is to move substantially up or down in any given time period. If the underlying pledged assets have been wisely invested and are increasing in value, a forced margin call becomes less likely, but you should still avoid using up too much of your capacity.

IMPORTANT TIP—KEEP AVAILABLE CAPACITY!

In a perfect world you would never draw more than 50 percent of your available capacity (on any line of any type), and the assets securing it would be positioned in a globally diversified portfolio that is prepared for a range of outcomes.

Typically, ABLFs will be set up with a cap and roll structure. Until you actually write a check off of the loan account checkbook or wire money out of it, you will not be charged any interest at all. But once you do access the account, interest will start accruing on a monthly basis. However, while you will be sent a monthly statement saying how much you have borrowed and how much interest has been generated, you are not required to pay off that interest or any portion of the principal. Month after month, if you so desire, you can simply let the interest accumulate, and there is no amortization that requires you to make a monthly principal payment. You do have to watch your coverage ratio (your available credit compared to your draw); if the amount you have borrowed gets too high, you might end up being in a forced margin call situation, depending on what is happening with the value of the pledged investments that are underlying your ABLF.[2]

As you establish an ABLF you will also want to be sure you understand if you are setting up what is called a purpose or nonpurpose loan. A *nonpurpose loan* is a line of credit or loan that is based on the eligible securities held in a brokerage account. They can be used for any suitable purpose except to purchase, trade, or carry securities or repay debt that was used to purchase, trade, or carry securities. Generally these funds cannot be deposited into a brokerage account (which can be problematic at times). A *purpose loan*, sometimes called a margin loan, is a revolving line of credit based on securities held in a brokerage account. Although these loans are primarily used to purchase securities, the proceeds can also be used for anything.

Finally, it's important to know that the interest rates charged on an ABLF are typically a combination of a standard index like the LIBOR (London Interbank Overnight Rate) plus a spread (with the spread being lower if you have pledged more assets and put a bigger ABLF into place). The total interest you are paying, therefore, floats in accordance with the LIBOR or other interest rate benchmark that was used.

If you are afraid that interest rates may go sky-high, one option that is usually offered is to fix all, some, or none of the loan (often starting at minimum amounts of $100,000), that is, to agree to a fixed interest rate for a certain period, typically one, three, five, or seven years. The downsides of doing this will depend on the firm and the economic environment, but they can include—and not necessarily be limited to—the following: potentially higher interest rates (greater cost), a prepayment or breakage fee for paying it off early, the requirement of monthly payments, and a balloon payment at the end of the multiyear period. A fixed-rate facility certainly gives you security knowing that you are protected from rates moving outside of your comfort zone. But it also decreases the Indebted Strength of Flexibility that the ABLF has provided you with in the first place. As with many other things, only you and your advisor working closely can correctly weigh the pros and cons as to your personal situation.

The Many Advantages of Having an ABLF in Place

It will be useful at this point to summarize some of the initial advantages of setting up an ABLF, which generally include the following (check with your firm to confirm details as loan terms and conditions can vary by institution and change over time):

- There are *no ongoing fees* associated with initiating an ABLF or keeping one in place.
- If you never draw on your ABLF, you will never pay any expenses of any type and it will never cost you anything. That is, setting up an ABLF is *not the same thing* as taking on new debt, but rather, should be thought of as increasing your Strategic Debt capacity.
- After you draw on your ABLF, *the only fee typically associated with it is simple interest*, calculated as the interest rate times the dollar amount that is drawn.
- There are generally *no prepayment penalties, no credit fees, no application fees*, and *no intensive underwriting process or costs*.
- Generally, the existence, status, and draw amount of your ABLF is not reported to the credit bureaus. Check with your firm for their specific details on credit reporting.
- There is *generally no required monthly payment*; you can allow the interest to accrue on the facility, which is also called *cap and roll*.[3]

Another way to look at the advantages of having an ABLF in place is in terms of the underlying financial distress model presented in Chapter 2 along with the detailed discussion of the four Indebted Strengths. Thus, when you make use of Strategic Debt in consultation with an informed advisor, you are given accessibility to the four Indebted Strengths of Increased Liquidity, Increased Leverage, Increased Flexibility, and Increased Survivability. As shown in the diagram describing the Smith family's situation in Chapter 3, the first thing taking on additional Strategic Debt gives you is Increased Liquidity, and out of that Increased Liquidity flows Increased Flexibility, and from this Increased Flexibility follows both Increased Leverage and Increased Survivability.

By putting an ABLF into place, you have Increased Liquidity, which, in the case of potential financial distress, enables you to avoid direct costs (like forced liquidation) or indirect costs (for example, debilitating worry and anxiety). In the case of responding to a serious storm—which we'll turn to shortly—this Increased Liquidity will enable you to rapidly make the repairs you need, and the Increased Flexibility that comes from your Increased Liquidity will let you make these repairs with cash in hand. This may be a better situation and could work to your favor in particular for short-term needs (especially if it is not a good time to sell from a market or tax perspective), or somehow else finding a way to rapidly come up with the necessary funds (which usually means taking on a loan at unfavorable terms). Increased Survivability also flows out of having the kind of cash you need, when you need it, to respond to a wide variety of natural, personal, and family-related situations.

The last Indebted Strength, Increased Leverage, also flows down to you from having the Increased Liquidity and Increased Flexibility

THE GREATEST DISADVANTAGE OF NOT SETTING UP AN ABLF

What is the biggest disadvantage of *not* putting an ABLF in place?

If you choose to not set up an ABLF, you are increasing the likelihood that you will experience substantial financial distress.

Specifically, in the case of a disaster, emergency, or family crisis—all of which can bring you to the doorstep of serious financial distress—you are exposing yourself to the potential of increased

- Direct costs (higher borrowing fees)
- Indirect costs (worry and anxiety)
- Duration (the crisis could last longer)
- Impact level (the crisis could hit you harder)

Put differently, putting yourself in a position—through your failure to take the simple steps necessary to put an ABLF into place—where you don't have access to a significant amount of ready, liquid funds is putting yourself in a position where you are much less able to effectively, flexibly, and sanely respond to future risks and dangers, seen and unseen.

associated with the ABLF. Depending on the type of line you have established, you may not be able to make additional financial investments with funds from the line. However, having money available gives you Increased Leverage in other ways, like the ability to invest in your business or the ability to pay down high-interest credit card loans at a much lower rate of interest.

Why Virtually Every Company Has a Line of Credit

As you will recall from Chapter 2, the second tenet of Strategic Debt Philosophy is to *explore* thinking and acting like a company. That doesn't necessarily mean that you should *act* like a company in all ways, but you should at least consider what companies are doing and why and see if similar strategies are appropriate for you based on your individual situation. Companies, unlike individuals or families, mainly exist for the purpose of making a profit, so it seems fair to assume that when it comes to financial matters, they have a pretty good idea of what they are doing. What, then, can be learned from companies when it comes to setting up a line of credit?

First, it should be said that while companies with large investment portfolios can set up ABLFs that look much like those used by individuals and families, companies usually set up other types of lines of credit that they can rely on during tough times or a disaster. These lines of credit are often set up against accounts receivable or inventory, and depending on the size of the company and the totality of its pledgeable assets (including such things as real estate and factory equipment), the owners of the company may be asked to personally guarantee a line of credit, something they may be loath to do. One way or another, though, most companies of any size have some kind of emergency line of credit that they can fall back on.

Now, in Chapter 2, the following question was asked: "If you are the CFO of a public company and you haven't focused on your optimal debt ratio, do you know what you would be?" The answer, of course, was that you would be *fired*. The same thing holds with regard to a company having a line of credit to fall back on.

If I were the president or CEO of a company and my CFO chose to not set up a line of credit, and then a need arose, what would I do?

I would immediately fire him or her!

The same concept applies to your need for a line of credit for your family. Like companies, it is just as important for individuals to consider having a line of credit in place.

Why, then, does nearly every company have some fallback line of credit in place?[4] Quite simply, because it's very important to at minimum have the Increased Liquidity, Increased Flexibility, Increased Survivability, and Increased Leverage associated with a line of credit. In this respect, companies and individuals or families are in exactly the same boat. Bottom line: Nearly every company has something like this in place, and you should too, especially given the ease of, and lack of costs involved in, putting an ABLF into place and the tremendous value it can have when something bad happens, as I experienced in 2008, which we'll now turn to.

Surviving Storms and Other Natural Disasters

In the world there is nothing more submissive and weak than water. Yet for attacking that which is hard and strong, nothing can surpass it.

—*Lao Tzu*

In 2008 one of the worst natural disasters in the history of the United States of America struck the Midwest. According to FEMA,

In Iowa numerous communities experienced flood crests exceeding historic levels, and some areas flooded well outside of the 1 percent annual-chance floodplain. Billions of dollars in damage occurred as homes, businesses, and critical facilities were inundated. In Cedar Rapids, a flood crest more than 12 feet higher than the previous record flooded areas well outside of the 1 percent annual-chance floodplain, inundating an area over nine square miles.[5]

Did you notice the part about Cedar Rapids? Cedar Rapids just happens to be my hometown, and while I do much of my business out of Chicago these days, I also keep a vibrant work and personal presence in Cedar Rapids, where members of my family have lived for six generations. Now, take a careful look at the picture in Figure 4.1—a picture of my Cedar Rapids office that was taken immediately after the flood and before any repairs were done. With my office on the first floor, you can see the force with which the water struck the building, pushing railroad ties and tress and other debris into the space, completely destroying everything. The strength of the current running through the office space removed all of the furniture, and did tremendous amounts of damage.

When something like this happens, how fast do you need money to make repairs and get going again? The answer, obviously, is "You need money immediately! You need money *now* because you need

Figure 4.1   A Picture of My Office after the Flood of 2008

to be cleaning out the existing space; ordering new furniture; putting down payments on temporary office space or on new office space entirely; ordering all new technology, from phone systems to computers and printers. You need money . . . now!"

While having insurance for this kind of natural disaster is also obviously important, it would be unrealistic to expect the insurance company to rapidly send you a check for $500,000 and tell you to go ahead and spend it on whatever you think is most important. With an ABLF in place, in this kind of situation—or one that affects your personal residence—you can be back in business much more quickly and effectively without having to liquidate part of your personal savings or take out a loan at very unfavorable rates.

The Criticality of Being Proactive and Assessing Risks

It is often said that timing is everything, and that's especially true with regard to an ABLF. If you try to set one up *after* a devastating storm or natural disaster has occurred, after the financial crisis has happened, after the life-threatening illness requiring immediate expensive surgery has happened . . . well, then it's typically too late. In any of these situations, in order to avoid having to liquidate assets in a haphazard and suboptimal manner, *you need money right away*.[6]

Keep in mind that under the best of circumstances it will typically take two to three weeks to set up an ABLF. Imagine, though, what would likely happen to that time frame in the days following a major disaster such as another super-storm or an earthquake. With increased demand for emergency money of all sorts, including that which can be derived from an ABLF, it is very likely that the time period before you could get the ABLF in place and accessible would be dramatically increased.

Now, you might think to yourself, "Look, I'm not going to encounter an emergency situation." But really, none of us can make that kind of statement. All of us face emergencies at one time or another. That's just part of life, and nothing will ever change that. Unfortunately, we all tend to have short memories; we all tend to

HURRICANE SANDY

Hurricane Sandy struck in 2012 and was one of the worst natural disasters in American history. According to the national Climatic Data Center the storm caused at least 60 deaths and $42 billion in property damage. Emergency managers recommended mandatory evacuations of more than half a million people who lived in low-lying areas. Widespread significant power outages impacted more than 2 million people and lasted two weeks.[7]

This storm is an example of many where large numbers of people are impacted so fast, so severely, and at the same time. Those who had access to credit were in a better position to use all of the Indebted Strengths: Increased Liquidity, Increased Flexibility, Increased Leverage, and Increased Survivability. You can't wait to set up a line of credit; you need to have one already set up.

think, "It won't happen to me"; and we all tend to have a substantial misunderstanding of the nature of risk, including *exogenous* risk, meaning originating from the outside or externally derived, versus *endogenous* risk, meaning proceeding from within or internally derived.

To help understand these two kinds of risk, please consider a case that I remember from business school. It involves the CEO of a manufacturing company with a plant in Boston. As it starts to snow one day, the CEO leaves the office. The next day he comes back and finds out that there was a giant blizzard overnight, with so much snow accumulating that the manufacturing plant's roof caved in. A lot of equipment was destroyed, and the plant had to be shut down for some weeks.

Most people—like this CEO—may think the blizzard was an *exogenous* shock, since after all, you can't control the weather! The CEO, who failed to take out insurance for this eventuality, felt he couldn't have anticipated a snowfall of this size. However, the moral of the case study is that what happened here was actually an *endogenous* event and risk, that is, a large snowfall in Boston should have been in the plant manager's base case scenario.

Since everybody knows that from time to time there are going to be very large snowfalls in Boston, the CEO should have had a plan to deal with this eventuality. Did he have the right roof? Did he have a snow removal service? Did he have a snow emergency plan? Did he have insurance or a line of credit in place for just such an eventuality? This disaster should have been mitigated or at least anticipated. Blaming it on Mother Nature isn't going to get the plant back in operation any sooner.

This case study has implications for both sides of your balance sheet. Both natural disasters and man-made ones will occur and, unfortunately, they will impact you. We can count on Mother Nature to generate tornadoes, earthquakes, fires, and floods that will destroy personal property, cars, and places of business, and in fact, we may see weather turning unexpectedly worse in ways we've never seen before. (For a great read on this subject, see *SuperFreakonomics: Global Cooling, Patriotic Prostitutes, and Why Suicide Bombers Should Buy Life Insurance* by Levitt and Dubner [2011].) On the man-made side of things, there may be wars, major fraud, and companies and industries could go suddenly bankrupt, throwing untold thousands out of work. The worst part of this is that over time, at least some of these things will not only happen to you; they will happen to your loved ones as well. Having an ABLF in place enables you to address the harsh real-world fallout from these situations in a much more effective and efficient manner.

Unfortunately, when reviewing the lists of natural and man-made problems listed here, many people tend to assume that certain shocks or events are exogenous—"I couldn't have possibly known this was going to happen!" The reality, however, is that almost any shock or disaster you can think of—and even those you can't articulate—*should be endogenous to your assumptions.* You need to assume that some or all of these things *will* happen, including some things that you never ever thought would happen, and that ultimately it is a question of when, not a question of if.

We can't see the black swan before it swims by; we can't anticipate the chunk of ice that falls off the airplane and destroys our roof; we can't know ahead of time that our sewer ejection pump will fail and that a toxic spill will happen in our home that will cost tens of thousands of dollars to remediate. But *we can know that some of these sorts of things, including things we never anticipated*, will in fact happen, and will happen to us and our family, friends, and loved ones.

Family Finances: First Bank of Mom and Dad; Elder Care Bridge Loan

An ABLF can come to the rescue not only in disaster-related situations, but also in family-related situations as well. Children, particularly those between 16 and 30, often don't maintain the cash reserves they should in case of an emergency. Many have less than one month's pay in hand, and all too often there is an equal (or greater) balance on a credit card or two. Such children can't handle a substantial financial shock. From a car accident to a medical emergency to a run in with the law—bail ain't cheap!—a parent (or parents) with an ABLF at their disposal has the ability to step in and help out the children when they need it most.

Having an ABLF available can also be mighty helpful in non-emergency situations involving children. One such situation is when the parents (or parent) of an adult child step in to help the young adult work through his or her debt or otherwise get off to a good or better start in life. It's not unusual for adult children to run up credit card debt in the tens of thousands of dollars. By using their ABLF, the parent or parents can step in, help the adult child clear up his or her debt, and essentially drop the interest rate that the adult child has to pay from the 18 or 20 percent zone to something that's less than a quarter of that. None of this will appear on the adult child's credit score. The adult child can then redirect monthly payments to paying down the ABLF, and the parents have the option to forgive the adult child's debt entirely at any point they want to. (Of course, the parent(s) would still be responsible for the debt and need to watch their coverage ratios.)

On the other end of the age spectrum, an ABLF lets the children of the elderly step in and seamlessly help them out when such help is needed. For example, many people who are between 80 and 90 may, at some point in time, need to move from their existing home into a care facility. But these units tend to be very competitive, and when a desirable unit in a quality care facility becomes available, you need to move on it immediately by putting down a substantial sum of money to secure the unit.

Suppose your dad passed away a few years ago, your mother is 87 years old and in failing health, and she suddenly needs $200,000 immediately to secure the care facility unit that is her top choice. Well, with an ABLF in place, your mother can use the ABLF as a bridge loan and pay off the debt when the house is sold. An ABLF gives you flexibility in these kinds of situations, enabling one's parents to get what they want or need in a way that isn't too onerous for anyone involved.

HELPING PARENTS, HELPING CHILDREN

Adult children can use their ABLF to create a bridge loan for a family member. This works up for elderly parents, such as in the preceding example, or down for children. An ABLF is one of the best ways that I know to easily bridge these scenarios. There can be tax and legal implications, so for these situations it is particularly important to consult with all of your professional advisors, including financial, accounting, and legal.

Taking Advantage of Opportunities and Distressed Sales

In addition to help protect you against bad times—against financial distress and its associated direct and indirect costs, impact level, and duration—an ABLF can also help you take advantage of specific opportunities, in bad times and good.

As a simple example, as shown in the chart on the Varieties of Debt in Appendix A, among the worst kinds of debt you can find yourself saddled with is expensive credit card debt. Suppose you have $50,000 of credit card debt. With the help of this book, and common sense, you soon realize that at an average interest of 18 percent, letting that credit card debt remain in place is quite a lot like throwing money down a hole.

Fortunately, if you are qualified and eligible and have an ABLF in place, you can borrow that $50,000 at a much lower rate (at 4 percent or lower as of the time of this writing). So, instead of having 18 percent interest payments that are due every month, you might end up with a 4 percent payment that you are not obligated to address every month.

Restructuring one's credit card debt is one way to seize an opportunity afforded by an ABLF. Another very different type of opportunity can come in the form of a distressed sale. Basically, the ABLF gives you the flexibility to buy what you want to buy, when you want to buy it, so if you see a great deal in front of you, you can seize the moment. For example, suppose you are looking for a new car and the one you want typically sells for $50,000. But the car dealer you've been speaking to has let you know that he himself has a cash flow crisis and that if you could pay with cash that very day, he would give you a $15,000 or 30 percent discount. You have looked around and know that this is a tremendous offer. Instead of wondering whether you have enough cash in hand, you simply call your financial firm and have them wire the dealer the $35,000 (or write a check from your checkbook), and then over the next few days you can sort out exactly how you want to pay for the car, what assets to sell if any, and whether to keep some, all, or none of the $35,000 on the line of credit. While that $35,000 draw would start generating a monthly amount of interest, there is a lot of flexibility in deciding how to deal with that debt because there are no required payments of interest or principal in most situations.

INSTANT ACCESS

I have seen numerous instances where a client had $50,000 in cash and a $1 million plus portfolio and wanted to buy a $50,000 plus car. Having the facility proactively in place enables the firm to wire the money right to the dealership. The advisor and client can later sit down together and determine how they want to pay for the car (what they want to sell and when they want to sell it).

Another realm where distressed sales representing extraordinary opportunities occasionally arise is real estate. An investor had a neighbor who had a vacant lot listed at $225,000. Over time the neighbor lowered the listing price to around $150,000. The investor approached the neighbor and said she would "give him $115,000 cash any time he wanted to sell it," and *within seven days the deal was done* with no under-writing, no inspection, and no mortgage lender involvement. The only reason it took as long as seven days was to conduct a title search and prepare the legal documents to transfer the deed. In this case, though, without the ABLF the investor would not have been able to step in immediately and close the deal. The client had as much time as she liked to decide how to—and how much of—the $115,000 to pay down.

Average ABLF Usage and the Win-Win-Win Scenario

The Certified Financial Planner recommendation is clear that one should set up lines of credit in good times and then access them in bad times.[8]

> Although many ABLFs are not used at any given point in time, most are used at some point in time.

My research based on informal surveys with leaders in banking throughout the industry indicates that as of the time of this writing, the majority of clients of large financial firms *do not* have an ABLF in place. Many large firms only have 10 percent of their clients with lines of credit in place—and several are well under that! This statistic is baf-fling, because as stated throughout this chapter, an ABLF costs nothing to put in place and nothing to use until you draw against it, and if it does come down to using it, it can literally be a lifesaver. As Richard Thaler suggests in the book *Nudge* (2009), we need to "change the default."[9] It *should* be that 90–100 percent of eligible clients have an ABLF in place. Whether you just simply see it as providing a substantial cushion in times of emergency or in times of opportunity, it makes a whole lot of sense to have one ready before the need is there.

Investors are rightly concerned about conflicts of interest in the financial services industry. One final interesting point about an ABLF is that it is beneficial for the individual investor/client, for the individual's financial advisor or private banker, and for the firm holding the pledged assets and establishing the credit facility. The advantages to the individual are obvious and have been discussed throughout this chapter.

As the case studies will illustrate, for the financial advisor, the advantages come mostly from being able to be a better—more holistic and ultimately effective—advisor who is able to manage both sides of the balance sheet. It enables an advisor to save his or her clients' money, and it should increase client satisfaction and therefore, retention.

Few people love financial firms these days, but it is also worth discussing the value of ABLFs to the firms that provide them. This type of loan represents traditional lending. I'll be so bold as to suggest that it is the type of business you want and expect a bank to be doing. There is nothing exotic or unusual about it—it essentially is just a traditional secured loan to existing clients. Troubles with the product traditionally come not from firms but from investors not following the advice outlined in this book (too high of a debt ratio, too much drawn on the line, collateral not globally diversified and positioned for a range of outcomes).

These lines are secured with client assets that are on deposit and are valued every day. Since the facility size is based on the value of the assets, they are very low risk to the financial firm. The rate is based on a spread over the firm's cost of capital. Once the financial firm has the platform in place to issue these facilities, there are almost zero incremental expenses (no additional real estate, people, computers, or technology). Therefore, a majority of the spread over the cost of capital becomes profit that drops right into the firm's bottom line. This is why even if the rate is relatively low, the firm is better off as well. It is also why ABLFs should offer you, as a qualifying individual or family, some of the best loan terms that are available.

Chapter 4: Summary and Checklist

While an ABLF was touched on in Chapter 2 as "The One Thing You Must Consider," this chapter discussed and analyzed ABLFs in detail, including what an ABLF is and how it works, why companies have an ABLF or something similar in place, the many advantages of having an ABLF, the importance of putting one in place *before* a disaster strikes, and how ABLFs can be used in a variety of situations, from natural disasters and emergencies to helping out family members to taking advantage of distressed sales and other extraordinary economic opportunities.

To put an ABLF into place, you have to pledge qualifying securities that you have on account with a financial institution. The amount of interest you are charged on your ABLF depends on how great a loan facility you put into place (which is based on the total amount of assets you are willing and able to pledge), with lower interest rates—usually a combination of a standard index like the LIBOR plus some additional percentage—attaching to facilities with greater total maximum draws. Once you make use of some portion of your ABLF—by having the money wired or by writing a check on your ABLF-linked checkbook—you start to accumulate monthly interest, but this is on a cap and roll basis, meaning there are no required monthly payments of interest or principal.

Importantly, it's best to reserve most or all of an ABLF for emergencies or substantial opportunities where having cash available immediately makes a big difference. If you use too much of your capacity and then there is a drop in the underlying value of the securities, there can be a forced margin call. This means the financial institution will sell some of your investments in virtually whatever manner it chooses to ensure it won't lose money. This is not something you ever want to have happen, so choose wisely when using your ABLF and in positioning your investments.

As you will see in the case studies, it is for this reason that we recommend that the majority of debt be structured versus homes, freeing the ABLF for flexibility and emergencies.[10] In a perfect world, you would not draw over 50 percent of your available credit, and the assets securing your line would be positioned in accordance with the themes in Appendix C.[11]

Checklist

❏ Do the basic mechanics of an ABLF—how you set one up, how interest is charged, how you use it to access liquid cash—make sense to you?

❑ Do you understand the cap and roll features, as well as what happens if you fix some or all of the money that you have accessed?

❑ Given the many advantages to setting up an ABLF and the fact that it costs you nothing at all until you access some of the money, do you see why it makes sense for virtually everyone who qualifies to set one up?

❑ If you have children or living parents, can you see how having an ABLF in place might afford you the opportunity to make a tremendous difference in their lives at relatively little cost to you?

❑ Do you understand the potential dangers of overusing your ABLF in terms of how it might eventually precipitate financial distress of its own and cause a forced margin call on your portfolio assets?

❑ Does calling an ABLF a win–win–win situation for you, your advisor, and his or her firm make sense to you?

Notes

1. A wide variety of securities may not count toward the amount you can borrow against with an ABLF. Such securities may include—but are not limited to—securities trading for under $10 a share, securities with a market capitalization of under $50 million, structured products, market-linked notes, and illiquid or thinly traded securities. Securities in tax-advantaged retirement accounts may also be ineligible. It is important that you work closely with your financial advisor or private banker to determine what securities are eligible for pledging and borrowing against. See Appendixes A, B, and C for additional details.

2. Coverage ratio is a measure of your available credit compared to your draw. As your assets fall, the available credit on your line falls as well. If I have a $1 million line of available credit with a $100,000 draw, then I am in a relatively low-risk situation. If I have a $900,000 draw on the same line, then I am in a relatively high-risk situation.

3. If you fix the interest rate on a substantial ABLF amount, typically $100,000 or more, you may indeed be taking on a kind of amortization, and monthly payments and a balloon payment at the end will probably be required. You may also incur a prepayment penalty if you pay off the fixed portion early.

4. Stephen A. Ross, Randolph Westerfield, and Jeffrey Jaffe, *Corporate Finance*, 10th ed. (New York: McGraw-Hill, 2013), 494–525, addresses this subject in detail.

5. www.fema.gov/library/viewRecord.do?id=3851.

6. If you have several months of cash on hand, as is recommended in the book, then that would be an additional source of liquidity that may or may not be

appropriate during an emergency. You would also have the ability to liquidate securities and would then have access to funds during traditional settlement periods. The use of cash, an ABLF, or liquidation should be discussed with your advisors at the time of need based on your individual circumstances.

7. www.ncdc.noaa.gov/stormevents/eventdetails.jsp?id=413124.

8. See Sections 8.42 and 8.43, Financial Planning Applications, in Craig W. Lemoine and Don A Taylor, eds., *Financial Planning: Process and Environment*, 3rd ed. (Bryn Mawr, PA: American College Press, 2009).

9. Richard H. Thaler, and Cass R. Sunstein, *Nudge: Improving Decisions about Health, Wealth, and Happiness* (New Haven, CT: Yale University Press, 2008).

10. This is not meant as an encouragement to borrow against your home and invest the proceeds but rather a statement that there are certain advantages to mortgage debt that need to be factored in to your decisions on what type of debt is best for you, if any. Understanding the benefits and risks of different kinds of debt is essential before choosing to implement these ideas.

11. The information in this chapter is to be considered in a holistic way as a part of the book and not to be considered on a stand-alone basis. This includes, but is not limited to, the discussion of risks of each of these ideas as well as all of the disclaimers throughout the book. The material is presented with a goal of encouraging thoughtful conversation and rigorous debate on the risks and potential benefits of the concepts between you and your advisors based on your unique situation, risk tolerance, and goals.

Part 3

SCENARIOS FOR SUCCESS

In the twentieth century, the United States endured two world wars and other traumatic and expensive military conflicts; the Depression; a dozen or so recessions and financial panics; oil shocks; a flu epidemic; and the resignation of a disgraced president. Yet the Dow rose from 66 to 11,497.

— Warren Buffett

Chapter 5

Long-Term Wealth Amplification through Capturing the Spread

The Basic Concept: Inherent Risks with Great Potential Rewards

Capturing the spread is a pivotal concept in Strategic Debt Practice and Philosophy. Capturing the spread refers to targeting and then capturing a return on investment that is higher than the cost of the debt—after taking into account all tax implications and transactions costs—that you take on to make that investment.[1] Put differently: Remember that Increased Leverage is one of the four Indebted Strengths that becomes available to you as part of Strategic Debt Practice. When you endeavor to capture the spread, then, you are using that Increased Leverage to attempt to make money on the money that you borrow.

But isn't this a risky practice? Borrowing money to make more money may seem foolhardy, and indeed, there are certain risks attached to it. There are no guarantees—and there can be no guarantees—that there will be a positive spread that can be captured. Any investment can go south, even those that seem rock bottom safe and secure. Things can always go terribly wrong.

For example, even if you are investing in apparently low-risk fixed-income instruments, the corporations, municipalities, or other governmental entities (domestic or foreign) whose bonds you hold could go bankrupt. If this happens, and you have borrowed against your ABLF, there might be a forced margin call on the account. In this way, you might end up increasing your risk of financial distress—as well as the potential direct and indirect costs, and potential impact level and duration of that financial distress—by having borrowed money to make money.

It's critical, then, that you come to terms with the fact that capturing the spread is inherently risky—regardless of how conscientious you are being—and could under some scenarios make your financial situation much worse in the long run. On the other hand, you have to weigh those kinds of possibilities against *the very real likelihood that the world as we know it will basically continue*, and that you could successfully accelerate your wealth accumulation for the long run if you are willing to take this risk. With this risk calculus in mind, the bottom line is for you to determine the following:

> Are there any investments, anywhere in the world, that you feel are highly likely to outperform the actual cost you are paying for the debt you would be taking on in order to capture the spread?[2]

If your answer is yes, then taking on additional debt probably makes sense—although there are a number of other factors that you also want to take into consideration. In the remainder of this chapter I will first consider some of these additional factors, and then provide some examples of how capturing the spread actually works and can benefit you. I will then expand Chapter 3's discussion of when to pay down debt, and when not to, in the context of maintaining an optimal debt ratio both now and in the future. I will then close the chapter by discussing how and why it is important to make sure that any efforts toward capturing the spread are in alignment with your overall investment strategy.

Three Key Factors to Consider

As just stated, the most important factor is whether after discussing matters with your advisor, you feel relatively comfortable and confident that you are going to be able to earn more on the money you borrow to make an investment than the actual, fully accounted for cost of borrowing that money. There are, however, three more factors that merit additional independent consideration. These are

1. The time horizon during which you hope to capture the spread, that is, how long a period of time are you looking at and working with. (Hint: The longer the time frame you have to work with, the more successful you are likely to be at capturing a positive spread.)
2. The resource base you are borrowing against and, therefore, the kind of debt and the interest rate you will be borrowing money at. (As the age-old saying goes, it takes money to make money, or put differently, it's relatively easier to become wealthier if you are already wealthy.)
3. Where you are with respect to achieving and maintaining an optimal debt ratio. If you are below your optimal debt ratio, then you have an additional incentive to take on appropriate debt.

Let's take these factors one at a time. First, with regard to *time horizon*, especially if you are investing in equities or other non-fixed-income products, the shorter the time frame you have, the chancier it will be that you will be able to successfully capture the spread.

Importantly, the goal is *not* to capture the spread every minute, every hour, or every day. There will obviously be some days that your account goes down while your debt continues to accrue interest. Moreover, extending this obvious proposition, there will be down months and even down years. The question, then, is what is a reasonable time period for evaluating whether you are successfully capturing the spread? Generally, a three- to five-year period seems to be a reasonable time to evaluate the success of the strategy.

At the end of a three-year period you can look back and determine if your portfolio returned an amount greater than your after-tax cost of capital. Keep in mind, if your net average cost of capital is 2.5 percent, then as long as your portfolio returned over 2.51 percent on a net basis, you have added value by having taken on an increased debt ratio.

In the event that you did not successfully capture a spread, you need to perform what is called an attribution analysis. This is an examination of where the strategy went wrong. Was it that there were no investments on earth that gave back a return greater than your cost of funds, or was it that you were not properly allocated to these investments? If you failed to earn a rate of return greater than your cost of debt, was the problem with the Strategic Debt Philosophy you were following, or was the problem with your investment strategy?

You certainly *can* lose money, and there are no guarantees. If you are lacking in skill, or are unlucky or careless, you might capture a *negative spread* where your rate of return is less than your cost of debt. Importantly, if you are making sensible investment allocation decisions, the longer the time frame you have to operate in, the greater your chances are of a positive outcome.

CAPTURING THE SPREAD FROM A CFO'S PERSPECTIVE

Companies will often have both cash on hand as well as outstanding debt. This cash will almost always have a rate of return less than their cost of debt, thereby earning a negative spread. Why do they do this? Why not just pay off their debt?

This cash acts as ballast for the company. Having cash and debt enables the company to better run both offense and defense with a range of outcomes in mind.[3]

It is essential to evaluate a strategy of capturing the spread across an entire portfolio rather than evaluating only by individual asset class. In fact, in a well-diversified portfolio—in any market environment—you should always have an asset that is underperforming your cost of capital. Portfolio managers call this negative correlation. Correlation, simply defined, is the way that assets move together. Traditionally, if the price of oil goes up, airline stocks go down (negative correlation); if a utility company goes up, other utilities tend to go up (this is positive correlation, as utility companies are largely very similar businesses); and if the price of corn goes down, then the price of a technology stock isn't likely to do anything in particular (this is zero correlation or probabilistic independence). Portfolio theory teaches us, among other things, that what matters more than the number of positions you have in a portfolio is the correlation between those positions.[4]

Many skeptical individuals might ask, "Well, how would this strategy have worked in 2008?" The answer of course is that it depends on what you owned at that time. If you were in global equities, then you likely captured a negative spread perhaps greater than −40 percent, depending on what you owned. If you were in certain areas of the bond market, you may have captured a positive spread of over 20 percent.[5] Also, we have to remember that many investors have the ability to go long or short on most asset classes. Just because an individual was under-owned an asset class or positioned the wrong way does not mean that the strategy was flawed; instead, perhaps it was the asset allocation that was flawed.

Table 5.1 looks at a three-year return series: 2007, 2008, and 2009. It assumes that you owned two assets—global bonds and global stocks—that hypothetically performed as shown.[6]

Table 5.1 Blended Returns 2007, 2008, 2009

	2007	2008	2009
Global bonds	10.7%	12.7%	1.4%
Global equities	11.7%	−46.7%	33.0%
50/50 portfolio	11.2%	−17.0%	17.2%
$1 million invested cumulatively	**$1,112,000**	**$922,960**	**$1,081,709**

This globally diversified portfolio had a cumulative return of approximately 8.2 percent (the investor in this example was up $81,709). If the investor had a positive spread, it likely would have been a nominal one, but the strategy was still effective or close to being effective during this period. Notice that stocks had an incredible negative spread in 2008, and that bonds had a negative spread in 2009 (1.4 percent was likely a lower return than their cost of capital). If we judged just the individual positions performance in a specific year we would likely make poor decisions and miss out on the wonderful benefits of low and negative correlation.

It cannot be stressed enough that you are not trying to capture a spread relative to every asset in your portfolio at every given point in time. You are not even trying to capture a spread relative to every asset over every 36-month period of time. Many, if not most assets go through 20 percent or more corrections given enough time. If you measure the performance in a short period of time, it could cause you to make very foolish decisions, including but not limited to selling assets at the exact wrong point in time.

The key, then, to measuring success is if your whole balance sheet, in aggregate, is growing at a rate of return greater than your net after-tax cost of capital over a three-year-plus time period. More importantly, as you look forward, you want to evaluate the strategy according to if you believe that your whole balance sheet will average a rate of return higher than your average after-tax cost of capital over the next three-plus years. Be cautious; it can be easy for investors to feel overconfident about their ability to outperform when the market is near new highs, and they may feel tempted to abandon the strategy near market lows.

The second factor concerns *the resource base you have*—your overall wealth level. The greater your resource base and the more wealth you start with, the easier it is going to be to capture the spread. This is easiest to see with regard to those who borrow money against their ABLF. You might intuitively question this statement mathematically, but it is true because your cost of capital changes as your assets grow.

If, for example, you pledge $5 million of taxable assets in setting up your ABLF, you will receive a much more favorable interest rate from your financial institution than if you have $500,000 to pledge. Thus, as this book is being written, the person able to pledge $5 million might only be charged a 2.5 percent interest rate, while the person with $500,000 to pledge might be charged a 4.5 percent interest rate. Those extra two percentage points make a huge difference in whether you are likely to reliably be able to capture a positive spread!

The level of your initial resource base will also affect the other types of debt you have available to you in the first place. If you haven't yet had a chance, please take a quick look at Appendix A, "The Varieties of Debt." Some kinds of debt are better than others, and perhaps the best kind of debt for a strategy such as this is real estate–related debt since it is tax advantaged. If you are in the 33 percent tax bracket and you can get a mortgage at 3 percent, then you are really only paying 2 percent for that money after your tax deduction. Essentially, if you are wealthy enough to take on a second home or property or qualify to refinance your present mortgage to a low interest rate—which you should be doing or have done anyway—then you are in a good position to attempt to capture the spread.

The third factor concerns where you are with regard to achieving and maintaining an optimal debt ratio generally, a subject that was discussed at some length in Chapter 3. We will revisit the idea of optimal debt ratios and future debt ratios later in this chapter. The basic idea, though, is that if you are below your optimal debt ratio—which is generally around 25 percent and will range from 15 to 35 percent—then you have an additional incentive to take on debt. Of course, if it doesn't seem to you that there are any investments anywhere in the world that you feel are highly likely to outperform (in aggregate and over time) the actual cost you would pay for the debt, then you should not do so. Where you are with regard to your ideal debt ratio, then, can be thought of not so much as a main determinant but rather as an additional factor to help you make up your mind in close cases before moving forward.

Some Scenarios for Capturing the Spread

To help better understand the ideas presented in this chapter, consider a scenario—we'll call this Jane Scenario A—where an individual named Jane is renting a house, has no material assets, and has just inherited

CAPTURING THE SPREAD—ADVANCED IDEAS

The term *anywhere in the world* that was expressed earlier is essential to consider as we move forward in the scenarios. Consider the following example: You borrow in your local currency (dollars) at 2 percent and invest in an international bond paying 3 percent. All else equal, if the dollar falls by 3 percent then your total return is 3% + 3% = 6% and you captured a spread of 4% (6% − 2%).

By borrowing in one currency and investing in another you are expressing a view with respect to that currency. This creates additional risk and return characteristics that are important to understand, especially with the experimental monetary policy that is occurring in many parts of the world.[7]

$1 million. Jane is debt averse and decides she wants to buy a home worth $500,000 outright, with no mortgage. This would leave her with a $500,000 investment portfolio. (It should be noted that one could arrive at the following balance sheet over time through any number of different ways outside of inheritance.) At this point Jane has no debt, no possessions valuable enough to include in these calculations, and a net worth of $1 million, as shown in the balance sheet in Table 5.2.

What about income? If Jane's investment portfolio returns an average of about 6 percent, she would be making roughly $30,000 in income per year, as shown in the income statement in Table 5.3. (For purposes of illustration, Jane's other income sources will be ignored. Also, all of the illustrations throughout the book are hypothetical and

Table 5.2 Balance Sheet—Jane Scenario A

Original Scenario A Balance Sheet

Assets		Liabilities
Real estate	$ 500,000	—
Investments	500,000	—
Total	1,000,000	—
Net worth	$1,000,000	**0% debt ratio**

Table 5.3   Income Statement—Jane Scenario A

Scenario A Portfolio Income

Portfolio		$500,000
Portfolio return	6%	30,000
After-tax cost of debt	0%	—
Net income from portfolio		**$ 30,000**

not intended to demonstrate the performance of any specific security, product, or investment strategy.)

Note that if the $500,000 she has in her portfolio completely consisted of pledgeable assets that she would be eligible for an ABLF of about $250,000.

Now let's consider a different scenario for Jane, that is, a different version of what her finances could have looked like had she made different choices along the way and embraced a Strategic Debt Philosophy. In this case, Scenario B, Jane could have purchased the same house with a mortgage of 80 percent loan to value, that is, a $400,000 mortgage. This would have allowed her to keep her money invested without having changed her net worth—unfortunately, you can't change your net worth through finance—Jane now has $1.4 million of assets and has a 29 percent debt-to-asset ratio ($400,000 divided by $1,400,000 equals about 29 percent), which is within the optimal debt ratio range. This is illustrated in the balance sheet in Table 5.4.

What happens to Jane from an income perspective in Scenario B? Assuming Jane has the same portfolio return of 6 percent, and assuming her mortgage was at a 3 percent rate and she is in the 33 percent tax bracket (so that the cost of that additional $400,000 in her portfolio

Table 5.4   Balance Sheet—Jane Scenario B

Scenario B Balance Sheet

Assets		Liabilities
Real estate	$ 500,000	$400,000
Investments	900,000	—
Total	1,400,000	$400,000
Net worth	$1,000,000	**29% debt ratio**

Table 5.5 Income Statement—Jane Scenario B

Scenario B Portfolio Income

Portfolio		$900,000
Portfolio return	6%	54,000
After-tax cost of debt on $400,000	2%	(8,000)
Net income from portfolio		$ 46,000
Additional income compared to A		**$ 16,000**

is effectively 2 percent, resulting in an $8,000 cost), then what happens to her net income? As the income statement in Table 5.5 shows, Jane now receives a net worth from her portfolio of $46,000, or $16,000 more than she received in Scenario A. So without having changed her net income, by taking on the mortgage at 3 percent she has increased her portfolio income by $16,000 a year, which is over 50 percent more compared to $30,000. (Of course, this is all assuming a hypothetical 6 percent portfolio return.) Note, too, that by taking on the mortgage debt Jane has increased her overall liquidity substantially, and she is now eligible for an ABLF of up to $450,000.

Another way to look at this is that while in Scenario A Jane would have to have over a 9 percent return on her investments to generate a $46,000 return ($500,000 × 9% = $45,000), in Scenario B Jane can get to the same place with just a 6 percent average return. There are obviously many more investments that are likely to reliably return 6 percent than those that will reliably return 9 percent. In fact, investments targeting 9 percent will almost certainly be more dangerous, more risky, and more volatile overall. This brings us to an important principle, which is the following:

Everything else being equal, a lower-volatility portfolio with debt is in many cases better than a high-volatility portfolio with no debt.

Similarly, a portfolio with no debt may actually be taking on more risk than a portfolio with debt yet achieving the same result.[8]

Without going into the mathematics here, let's just say that this principle is completely consistent with what is known as Modern Portfolio Theory and the Capital Allocation Line, and moreover, it just makes sense. Put differently, if you need a certain income from your portfolio, attempting to obtain that income with high-yielding investments also tends to greatly increase your risk, because the volatility associated with such investments means that things could go down, and go down a lot, and when you throw in the power of compounding and the effect of the order of returns—it makes a big difference whether things go down first and then up or up first and then down—you are a lot better off if you can bring more money to the table through the strategic use of debt and then target a lower, less-volatile return.

Comparing these scenarios side by side in Table 5.6 makes it clear that Scenario B is the more optimal scenario for Jane.

Let's consider two more scenarios for Jane. In Scenario C, Jane has not taken on a mortgage, but she has used her ABLF to pay for different

Table 5.6   Jane Scenario A and Scenario B: Side-by-Side Comparison

Existing—Jane Scenario A			Optimal Jane Scenario B		
Assets		**Liabilities**	**Assets**		**Liabilities**
Real Estate	$ 500,000	—	Real Estate $ 500,000		$ 400,000
Investments	500,000	—	Investments	900,000	—
Total	1,000,000	—	Total	1,400,000	400,000
Net worth	$1,000,000	**0% debt ratio**	Net worth $1,000,000		**29% debt ratio**
		Income Perspective			
Portfolio income	6%	$30,000	Portfolio income	6%	$54,000
After-tax cost of debt	2%	—	After-tax cost of debt	2%	(8,000)
Net Income		$30,000	Net Income		$46,000
			Additional income compared to scenario A		$16,000

CASH-OUT REFINANCE TO GET TO OPTIMAL?

This begs the question if I am implying that Jane should do a cash-out refinance to get to optimal. This is complicated as theory meets behavioral finance. The success of the strategy is always based on your ability to capture the spread, so mathematically, if you own your house outright and you feel you can capture the spread, you could consider taking on a mortgage to get to optimal. The problem with this is that the proceeds come to you as a lump sum and therefore you are very dependent on market returns at that exact moment. Mathematically this, of course, is no different than the situation Jane B finds herself in today, but psychologically it is different. You go from owning your house to the risk associated with capturing the spread.

An additional problem is that even if you wanted to do this, it is understandably frowned upon by many institutions and outright prohibited by others. It is my strong preference for many reasons that rather than do a cash-out refinance, individuals visualize their future debt ratios and work toward them along the way. This is accomplished by not paying down debt and instead building up a portfolio in a consistent, systematic way. In the financial industry we call this dollar cost averaging.

expenses—from taxes to vacations—and has saved the difference. Her CPA advises her that the interest on her ABLF is not tax deductible. Is this a good move compared to taking on the mortgage? The balance sheet in Table 5.7 shows Jane's situation.

We are still assuming a 6 percent return on her portfolio, and since the additional $250,000 is on a relatively small ABLF, we will also assume that she will be charged about 4 percent for that money. The income statement in Table 5.8 shows her income.

On the one hand, Jane is still up $5,000 a year compared to Scenario A. On the other hand, it is pretty clear that Scenario C— with a 20 percent debt ratio ($250,000 divided by $1,250,000) is

Table 5.7   Balance Sheet—Jane Scenario C

Scenario C Balance Sheet

Assets		Liabilities
Real estate	$ 500,000	—
Investments	750,000	$250,000
Total	1,250,000	$250,000
Net worth	$1,000,000	**20% debt ratio**

IS ABLF INTEREST TAX DEDUCTIBLE?

This is an excellent question and unfortunately it is a bit of a hornet's nest. You need to work closely with your tax advisor to determine the right answer for your situation. Some CPAs suggest that the IRS uses tracing rules so that it depends on the use of the proceeds. For example, if the proceeds are used to fund a business, then the interest may be a deductible business interest expense. Some say that if the use of the proceeds can be classified as a purpose facility, then it can be deducted as margin interest. Others say the interest would not be deductible in this situation.

---

nowhere near as desirable as Scenario B, with a 29 percent debt ratio. Why? Well, Jane is borrowing less money (gaining less Increased Leverage) for her portfolio, she is borrowing money at a more

Table 5.8   Income Statement—Jane Scenario C

Scenario C Portfolio Income

Portfolio		$750,000
Portfolio return	6%	45,000
After-tax cost of debt on $250,000	4%	(10,000)
Net income from portfolio		$ 35,000
Additional income compared to A		**$ 5,000**

Table 5.9   Balance Sheet—Jane Scenario D

Scenario D Balance Sheet

Assets		Liabilities
Real estate	$ 500,000	$400,000
Investments	1,350,000	450,000
Total	1,850,000	$850,000
Net worth	$1,000,000	**46% debt ratio**

expensive interest rate (4 percent versus 3 percent), and after taking into account that there is no interest deduction on ABLF-based debt, her after-tax cost of capital is 4 percent versus the 2 percent it was in Scenario B.

Let's consider one final scenario for Jane, Scenario D, a combination of Scenarios B and C. As the balance sheet in Table 5.9 shows, here she has taken on a $400,000 mortgage, bringing the portfolio to $900,000, and then taken out an ABLF in the form of a margin loan against her portfolio for $450,000 that her CPA advises will cost her 3 percent after taxes. This brings her total investments to $1,350,000. As a result she has a much larger asset base of $1,850,000. Of course, as shown in Table 5.9, Jane's net worth remains $1,000,000 ($1,850,000 − $850,000 = $1,000,000).

What happens to Jane's income? Consider the income statement in Table 5.10.

Table 5.10   Income Statement—Jane Scenario D

Scenario D Portfolio Income

Portfolio		$1,350,000
Portfolio return	6%	81,000
After-tax cost of debt on $400,000	2%	(8,000)
After-tax cost of debt on $450,000	3%	(13,500)
Net income from portfolio		$ 59,500
Additional income compared to A		**$ 29,500**

Here, Jane's total net portfolio income is now up to $59,500, or almost twice as much as the $30,000 in Scenario A. But despite this rosy outcome, this would probably not be a recommended course of action for Jane to take. Why not? If you recall, in Scenario B, Jane's debt ratio was 29 percent, a little higher than the ideal ratio of 25 percent, but certainly well within the 15–35 percent range. And in Scenario C, her debt ratio was only 20 percent, again within the range but perhaps a little low.

In this final Scenario D, however, Jane's debt-to-asset ratio is $850,000 divided by $1,850,000, or roughly 46 percent. Recall that we have been assuming 6 percent returns all along, but in reality markets don't move that way. Let's look back at the Table 5.1, Blended Returns 2007, 2008, 2009, from earlier in this chapter on capturing the spread. Notice in Table 5.11, if her investments were down 17 percent and the value of her house fell by 10 percent, her net worth would fall by $300,000 or about 30 percent!

Worse yet, if she was not properly diversified in her portfolio, she could have faced a much worse outcome, such as a 35 percent correction in her portfolio. Table 5.12 shows that due to the leverage she was using, this would have led her to a $544,000, or 54 percent, loss!

There's no doubt about it: In Scenario D, Jane's debt is just too high. Such a debt ratio drives up the real likelihood of Jane encountering substantial financial distress, increasing the direct and indirect costs of that financial distress, and also lengthening the duration and raising

Table 5.11   Too Much Debt in a Market Correction

Too Much Debt in a Market Correction

Portfolio		$1,350,000
Portfolio return	−17%	(229,500)
Change in the value of $500,000 house	−10%	(50,000)
After-tax cost of debt on $400,000	2%	(8,000)
After-tax cost of debt on $450,000	3%	(13,500)
Net change in the portfolio		**$ (301,000)**

Table 5.12 Too Much Debt in a Market Correction and Not Diversified

Too Much Debt and Not Diversified

Portfolio		$1,350,000
Portfolio return	−35%	(472,500)
Change in the value of $500,000 house	−10%	(50,000)
After-tax cost of debt on $400,000	2%	(8,000)
After-tax cost of debt on $450,000	3%	(13,500)
Net change in the portfolio		**$(544,000)**

TWO IMPORTANT NOTES:

1. Notice in all three scenarios Jane's net worth is constant at $1 million. Why? Because . . .

You cannot change your net worth through financing.

2. There is no change in the value of her house in each scenario. Any value change would have the same impact across each scenario. The value of an asset is completely independent of the financing around that asset—a topic that will be addressed in detail in the next chapter.

---

the impact level of that financial distress. Put differently, while Scenario D might seem desirable on some level, it is just too risky.

All of this brings us back to a central point made many times throughout this book. What has been provided here are merely examples of the dynamics involved with Strategic Debt Practice and Philosophy. To make sure you are doing the right thing for yourself and your family, you should without a doubt consult with an informed, open-minded, financial advisor before actually implementing any of these ideas. And you should have a very real sense of the potential risk that you are opening yourself up to by taking on increased debt.

Synching with Your Investment Strategy

Knowledge is power, and knowledge of Strategic Debt Philosophy and Practices can enable you to consciously take advantage of your four Indebted Strengths (Increased Liquidity, Flexibility, Leverage, and Survivability), which is a very good thing. However, any use of the ideas and practices in this book must, for your own good, take place *within the context of your overall sensible investment strategy*. Put differently, while Strategic Debt Philosophy and Practices can make a huge addition to your financial well-being in the long run, it's important to make use of them in the context of a well-thought-out financial plan and investment strategy. That is, while the ideas comprising Strategic Debt Philosophy and Practice are both important and practical and may make a major difference in your life, you wouldn't want to move forward in implementing them without considering the entirety of your financial and investment situation.

To that end, please consider the information in Appendix C ("No Guarantees: Limiting the Risks of Investing in a Crazy World"). Here it is suggested not only that you adopt a long-term goals-based approach to asset allocation, but also that you play both offense and defense, that you make sure you have the right kind of account structure in place, that you consider adopting a world-neutral view of investing (since there are opportunities across the globe), that you have your portfolio stress-tested against different economic scenarios, and that you never underestimate the importance of having liquid cash available at a moment's notice. Describing any of this in detail is far beyond the scope of this book, but you should at minimum make sure you are working with someone who knows what your hopes, dreams, and goals are, and who has a cogent rationale for how he or she can help you achieve them.

Chapter 5: Summary and Checklist

This chapter looked closely at the idea of *capturing the spread* for long-term wealth amplification. Essentially, capturing the spread involves borrowing money and then investing that money. The goal is to make a

ARE YOU PREPARED FOR THE FUTURE?

The Next 30 Years Cannot and Will Not Look the Same as the Last 30[9]

Many financial advisors and private bankers advise their clients as if the next 30 years will be pretty much the same as the last 30 years, but this simply is not and cannot be true. Instead, it is better to conceive of three distinct time periods:

1. The past 30 years
2. Today (now)
3. The next 30 years

Assume that each of these periods is unique and that most of the data from previous periods not only cannot repeat itself, but in many cases, could turn to the opposite over the next 30 years.

For example, in the last 30 years or so, from 1980 to 2013, we have seen

- Interest rates move from very high to very low.
- Inflation move from very high to low.
- U.S. government debt move from low to very high.

These types of macro-economic changes are either highly unlikely to repeat themselves or simply can't repeat themselves; for example, with the federal funds rate—what the government charges to banks—near or at zero, interest rates just can't go very much lower. There is a very real possibility that rates could eventually go higher or perhaps much higher. Whether or not interest rates still nudge down a bit, it's clear that the larger economic phenomena of rates moving from midteens to the 2 percent (and lower) range cannot repeat itself.

Unfortunately, many investors tend to use the last 30 years as the basis for their investment decisions. While history is informative and can point out general directions and trends, when dealing with risk it is better to start by essentially throwing out that data set (or considering it one of many data sets) and instead broadly

(Continued)

consider all alternatives and scenarios when attempting to discern what the future might plausibly look like and, more importantly, what to do in the present.

What's most important is to recognize that today we are in a completely different time period than we have ever been in before. If you are a U.S., Japanese, European, or Chinese investor, your starting place is not and cannot be the same as it has been in the past, which is why historic data needs to be used cautiously. And the 30 years that follow from today are highly likely to be full of both endogenous risks that come to pass and exogenous risks and shocks that we had never thought of. In fact, perhaps the single most important lesson from history is that things stay the same until they don't—a shift that often happens with blinding speed and surprising repercussions —and that we (including our national leaders) have control until we (and they) don't.

For example, we could very easily find ourselves in an environment of rising interest rates, falling GDP (gross domestic product), falling equity prices, and falling housing prices. And we could even find ourselves facing a long-term catastrophic failure of the U.S. government's finances, and therefore perhaps even the U.S. government itself.

It is certainly clear that we face huge challenges and that each of us needs to be prepared for a much wider potential range of outcomes as we move forward, especially if you are interested in trying to earn a rate of return greater than your cost of debt. I know that I don't always read all of the appendixes to a book, but I would encourage you to read Appendix C and really "get" the following:

- Changes are abrupt: Things are the way they are until they are not.
- By definition, we cannot see, expect, know about, or effectively plan for truly exogenous (outside) risks; again, we do not know what we do not know, and in fact, we cannot know what we cannot know.

(Continued)

ARE YOU PREPARED FOR THE FUTURE? (*Continued*)

- Changes in the status quo (for example, in the countries previously mentioned) were not desired by those who perceived themselves to be in control. Put differently, major changes will continue to happen in countries throughout the world despite the efforts of those in charge to prevent them, and there's no guarantee etched in stone that the United States of America won't undergo substantial changes in its political, economic, and social systems.

return that is higher than the cost of that debt. The vast majority of the population has some form of debt and is therefore attempting to capture the spread. The goal of this chapter is to explore how to do it in the most strategic way possible. This is an inherently risky strategy, and you should be well aware of the risks before you attempt it.

Important factors to consider when deciding whether to borrow money and then attempt to capture a positive spread include time horizon (the longer you have, the more likely you'll be successful), the resource base you are borrowing against and the interest rate you will be charged, and where you are with respect to achieving and maintaining an optimal debt ratio.

Finally, we considered the importance of synching any activities around capturing the spread with your overall investment strategy and portfolio plan. We proved that everything else being equal, a lower-volatility portfolio with debt is better than a high-volatility portfolio with no debt. This concept has tremendous implications on your overall investment strategy and should be discussed in detail with your advisors.[10]

Checklist

❑ Are you clear about the basic concepts behind capturing the spread?
❑ Do you understand that capturing the spread always involves some risk, and there are no guarantees that you will capture a positive

spread, but may in fact lose money on any investment and thereby capture a negative spread?

❑ Do the three key concepts of time horizon, resource base and cost of debt, and where you stand with relationship to maintaining an ideal debt ratio make sense to you?

❑ Did the four scenarios that were provided succeed in illustrating for you different ways that capturing the spread can actually be put into effect?

❑ Do you understand the math on how everything else being equal, a lower-volatility portfolio with some debt is better than a high-volatility with no debt?

❑ Are you clear about why it is so important to synch your investment strategy and long-term financial planning with any activities related to capturing the spread?

Notes

1. Going forward, your actual cost of debt will be defined just as it has been in this first paragraph, that is, the cost of debt to you after all tax implications and transactions costs are considered and taken into account.

2. Stephen A. Ross, Randolph Westerfield, and Jeffrey Jaffe, *Corporate Finance*, 10th ed. (New York: McGraw-Hill, 2013), Chapter 18. Pages 494–525 address this subject in detail.

   Companies do this as explained in "Valuation and Capital Budgeting for the Levered Firm." It is worth noting that companies often invest in many projects at the same time. Although they would like to, they know that they are taking risk and it is all but certain that they will not capture the spread on every investment individually. Some of their investments will be winners and some will be losers.

   See also Ziv Bodie, Alex Kane, and Alan Marcus, *Investments*, 9th ed. (New York: McGraw-Hill, 2011), Section 12.1, "The Behavioral Critique in Investments," and Chapter 19.

3. Ross, Westerfield, and Jaffe, *Corporate Finance*, Part VII, "Short Term Finance," addresses this subject in detail.

4. Bodie, Kane, and Marcus, *Investments*, Chapters 6 and 7.

   Harry Markowitz, "Portfolio Selection," *Journal of Finance*, March 1952.

5. http://research.stlouisfed.org/publications/regional/10/07/treasury_securities.pdf; www.standardandpoors.com/indices/sp-500/en/us/?indexId=spusa-500-usduf--p-us-l--.

6. All of the returns are hypothetical and not intended to demonstrate the performance of any specific security, product, or investment strategy. The case studies presented are for educational and illustrative purposes only and do not indicate future performance. Past performance is no guarantee of future results. Investment results may vary. The investment strategies and products and services presented are not appropriate for every investor. Individual clients should review with their financial advisors the terms and conditions and risks involved with specific products or services. Neither the information provided nor any opinion expressed constitutes a solicitation for the purchase or sale of any security.

7. See Bodie, Kane, and Marcus, *Investments*, Chapter 23 and Chapter 25, "Applied Portfolio Management International Diversification of Investments," for a complete discussion on this topic.

8. Bodie, Kane, and Marcus, *Investments*, Chapter 7.

9. The notion that there are three distinct periods in time—the past 30 years, today, and the next 30 years—is inspired from a presentation given by Jeffrey Rosenberg, Chief Investment Strategist for Fixed Income, BlackRock, at the Barron's Top 100 Conference, Fall 2012. Lectures from David Wessel, Luigi Zingales, Ed Lazear, and Martin Feldstein in the Fall of 2012/Winter of 2013 inspired some of the views expressed in this section. Readers looking for additional detail should read the following: www.imf.org/external/pubs/ft/weo/2012/02/pdf/c3.pdf; http://blog-imfdirect.imf.org/2013/01/23/we-may-have-avoided-the-cliffs-but-we-still-face-high-mountains; www.imf.org/external/pubs/ft/GFSR/index.htm; www.whitehouse.gov/omb/budget; www.treasurydirect.gov/govt/reports/pd/feddebt/feddebt_ann2012.pdf; http://cbo.gov/sites/default/files/cbofiles/attachments/43907-BudgetOutlook.pdf; http://online.wsj.com/article/SB10001424127887323353204578127374039087636.html.

10. The information in this chapter is to be considered in a holistic way as a part of the book and not to be considered on a stand-alone basis. This includes, but is not limited to, the discussion of risks of each of these ideas as well as all of the disclaimers throughout the book. The material is presented with a goal of encouraging thoughtful conversation and rigorous debate on the risks and potential benefits of the concepts between you and your advisors based on your unique situation, risk tolerance, and goals.

Chapter 6

Holistic Financing of the Expensive Things You Need and Want

A Better Way to Buy: In the Company of Holistic Financial Thinkers

While it is said that money can't buy you love, there's no question that we need money to buy pretty much everything else. This includes, but isn't necessarily limited to:

- The necessities of life, such as food, shelter, clothing, and medicine.
- Durable items and assets, such as appliances and automobiles.
- Major home improvements, such as a new roof or a new kitchen.
- Luxury items, such as high-end cars and boats, fine jewelry, and collectibles like paintings, antiques, or rare coins.
- Real estate, including second and vacation homes.

Returning for a moment to the *What would a company do?* metaphor that was made use of in Chapter 1, consider what happens when a company needs to buy new desks for all of its employees. Does the CFO of the company walk down the street to the nearest bank and say, "Please tell us about your desk financing options?" and then accept whatever interest rate the bank is willing to offer for a loan at that moment? Of course not!

Instead, the CFO looks at the entirety of the company's balance sheet—its assets and its liabilities—and then considers all of the plusses and minuses of all of the different financing options available. The CFO wants to determine the best way to finance the desks, which means determining the lowest cost of capital that will accomplish the company's objective. It's a holistic and pragmatic approach, one that considers all of the available loan and financing options in the context of what will be best for the company in the long run.

As an individual or family with some resources and wealth behind you, is there any conceivable reason why you wouldn't want to take the same approach? While it may be true, as discussed in Chapter 1, that individuals and families are not companies and ultimately may have very different kinds of goals than companies have, there's nothing virtuous about not being as smart with your money as possible, including when you are buying expensive items.

This chapter, then, will consider the options available to you when you want to buy something—in particular, expensive items. Let us start by looking at four basic principles and then consider specific scenarios that illustrate how you might buy a boat, or a car, or a diamond ring, or a second (or even a first) home. The most important thing to keep in mind is that by following Strategic Debt Principles and using Strategic Debt Practices to purchase expensive items, you continue to take advantage of your Indebted Strengths, effectively leveraging off of the different types of credit available to you, and thereby ultimately reducing the likelihood you will encounter severe financial distress (or if you do encounter it, that the direct and indirect costs of that financial distress, its severity, and its duration, will all be minimized).

Four Principles When Financing the Purchase of a Desired Item

There are four principles that you should keep in mind when considering how to finance the purchase of an expensive item. These are

1. The value of an item is 100 percent independent of the financing you have around that item.
2. Amortization stinks!
3. A fixed rate on a loan is similar to a form of insurance. Like all insurance you need to determine the cost of that insurance, and then compare it to the value you would receive versus your ability to self-insure.
4. Prior to making your purchase, seek out a qualified financial advisor who believes in holistic wealth management and who understands the concepts of strategic debt and optimal debt ratios.

The first principle concerns *the relationship between the type of financing you use to acquire an item and the value of that item.* Now, suppose the car you own is a late model BMW. The value of that car—the actual worth of the car—remains the same whether you bought it with cash from your savings, came up with the money through your ABLF, or took out a loan from the bank to purchase the car. Put differently, the structure of the financing, if any, used to acquire an item is 100 percent independent of the value of that item.

The value of an asset is 100 percent independent of the financing in place around that asset.

If you wanted to buy my house, you would not ask about the amount or terms of my mortgage. Similarly, if I go to sell my car, a prospective buyer wouldn't care if I owned it outright or had a loan against it.

The value you will receive upon selling an asset has nothing to do with whether that asset has a loan against it.

Another way to think of it is in terms of the following question: If you have a car loan today and then you pay off that loan tomorrow, does the value of your car change? The answer, of course, is no. The car would be worth exactly the same today as it was worth yesterday (except perhaps it might be worth a tiny bit less because there is one more day of depreciation that has to be subtracted from its value). Similarly, your house—or your second house or vacation home or a Renaissance painting or a rare coin collection—will either appreciate in value or depreciate in value regardless of the financing you have in place around it. Delinking the type of financing and the value of an item is an important root principle that allows us to think better— more holistically, more creatively—about the varieties of financing available to you.

The second principle put plainly and simply is that *amortization stinks*! Amortization requires the borrower to repay parts of the loan over time. What is the problem with this? If you take on a loan with amortization that means you will have *an inflexible minimum monthly payment* that you have to make (including both interest and principal reduction) no matter what else is going on in your life. This cuts directly against the Indebted Strength of Increased Flexibility and also amounts to *decreased* liquidity just when you might need it the most. A loan with amortization locks you in until that loan is paid off, ties up capital in fixed assets, and reduces your savings—which is why you should avoid such loans whenever possible. Even items that are considered depreciating assets—which are necessarily worth less as every year goes by—can be financed interest only. There is no need to link such a depreciating asset with an amortization schedule.

One hundred percent of all publicly traded corporate debt in America is issued on an interest-only basis.[1]

Let's return for a moment to how companies think and act, and ask yourself if you have ever purchased an amortizing corporate bond, one where you receive monthly interest payments as well as a locked-in portion of the principle being paid back to you on a monthly basis. The answer is no, you haven't ever purchased such a bond, because 100 percent of corporate debt in America is issued on an interest-only basis (with the principal paid at the bond's call date or maturity). If I purchase a bond from General Electric or Walmart or IBM, I will receive an interest payment every six months, but I will never receive a principal repayment until the bond matures.

So if companies only issue interest-only nonamortizing bonds, then why do individuals agree to amortizing car loans, boat loans, home loans, and so on?[2] Harkening back to the pervasive knee-jerk antidebt stance that most people have, perhaps the willingness to agree to amortizing loans has to do with the idea that this is a quicker and guaranteed way to be debt free at the end of the day. Certainly, however, no CFO of any company would agree to amortization unless absolutely forced to, because agreeing to a fixed monthly payment *no matter what else is happening in your life* increases your risk of encountering financial distress and increasing its costs (direct and indirect), its duration, and its impact level.

Think about it: Whether you're in good times or bad times, if you have an amortizing loan, you are required to make the same monthly payment *no matter what*. If you have a nonamortizing way of financing the purchase of an expensive item, then when times are bad you can make little or no payment, but if you get a big bonus, then you can decide to pay down some, most, or all of the remainder of the loan (of course taking into account where you are with respect to your optimal debt ratio).

> An amortization schedule reduces your flexibility in good times and bad, which is just when you will need that flexibility the most!

This point is so important it is worth repetition through a quick example. Suppose you have a $500,000 home loan at 4 percent amortizing over 15 years. Your monthly payment would be roughly $3,700 per month. If you pay down $250,000 your next month's payment is . . . the exact same amount! What if you lose your job? Your next month's payment is still $3,700 and there is nothing you can do to change it.

The bottom line is that you should avoid amortization whenever possible, which means avoiding many commonly commercially available and bank-originated loans and financing options whenever possible.

ONE OF THE WORST FINANCIAL DECISIONS I SAW SOMEBODY MAKE . . .

Perhaps one of the worst financial decisions I saw an individual make was to purchase a vacation home on a 15-year amortizing loan. It wasn't the purchase price, but as an outside observer I was stunned when I heard she chose an amortizing loan.

She was an executive with a high income and a seemingly unassailable career. Well, wouldn't you know it, about two weeks later she lost her job in a corporate reorganization, and suddenly she had to come up with the money to pay for both her main home and the vacation home.

With sky-high payments she had to liquidate many of her assets to pay for the second home, thus experiencing an intensified level of financial distress, including higher direct and indirect costs of this financial stress. Of course this forced liquidation was happening during a rotten time in the market.

Far too often those with big incomes take on a second car, a second home, or other expensive items through financing that includes amortization, and more often than you might guess, they end up greatly regretting this.

Many people might say, "Wait a second! Are you saying I should have interest-only debt on my car? But my car *will* depreciate over time." Here principles 1 and 2 come together. Just because an asset depreciates does not mean that you need to have an amortization schedule for it. Moreover, with an interest-only loan I can choose to pay down any amount of principal any time I want to. Think about it from a CFO's perspective. Do companies own assets that depreciate? Absolutely! If a large company owns 50,000 desks that are good for, say, 10 years, they don't go out and issue a desk bond that amortizes over 10 years. They issue debt based on their whole balance sheet, knowing that some of their assets will appreciate over time and some of them will depreciate over time.

The third principle is that *loans with fixed interest rates represent a form of insurance*. Like all insurance you need to quantify the cost of the insurance versus the potential benefits and your ability to self-insure. A fixed rate is similar to an insurance policy against the risk of rising rates in the future. Clearly there are many advantages to fixed-rate debt, especially in a rapidly rising interest rate environment. Depending on your personal circumstances, your economic view of the world, or the current interest rate environment, buying such insurance might not be a bad thing—in fact it might be the smartest thing to do! That said, you should always consider the extra cost of that insurance versus your ability to self-insure against the risk of rising interest rates, especially because in most (but not all) economic times, loans with floating (i.e., nonfixed) rates tend to embody the lowest cost of capital at any given moment.

MAKING THE WRONG CHOICES

So often what I find is that individuals who can afford the risk of floating-rate debt are set on having fixed-rate debt, and individuals that should have fixed-rate debt choose floating-rate debt.

Those who can afford to self-insure don't choose floating-rate loans, and those who can't afford to self-insure do choose floating-rate loans.

If you choose floating-rate debt based on the rate, then be sure that you have your floating risk insured in some way. Floating-rate debt can easily increase your risk and cost of financial distress.

Like so many things that have been discussed here, more often than not people choose the exact opposite of what would be optimal for their situation.

Many of us choose fixed-rate mortgages because we want the peace of mind that goes along with knowing that the interest rate on the mortgage won't go higher. So if you are buying a vacation home and have the option to choose between 2 percent interest-only LIBOR floating loan and a 5 percent 30-year fixed loan, you might choose to go with the 5 percent rate so that you don't have to worry about fluctuating interest rates. The difference between the two rates is 3 percent (5% − 2% = 3%). If this is a $1 million property, this difference amounts to a $30,000 pretax difference per year.

In essence, then, this is a sort of insurance policy against rising interest rates. But $30,000 per year is pretty expensive insurance! If instead of paying this "insurance premium" you choose to go with the 2 percent interest-only LIBOR floating-rate mortgage, you can technically self-insure and save this premium.[3] You are now in a position to manage your payments, and if at any time you feel that rates are going to rise precipitously, you can either pay down or refinance the mortgage (of course, at then-prevailing interest rates, which could be higher). You can save a great deal in the long run, especially if you end up selling the property early on in the 30-year time frame. (Many agents tell me the average length of time that any given individual keeps any given piece of property is only about seven years.)

Let's stress-test this scenario: If you choose to go for the floating interest rate and interest rates then rise from 2 percent to 3 percent, you are still ahead. If they rise to 4 percent, you are still ahead. If they rise to 5 percent, it is a push. You are not behind until rates rise above the cost of the fixed rate. At that point in time you can step in and pay it off. Keep in mind that if you embrace all of the ideas in this book— and it is important to remember that they all go together—by having a debt ratio around 25 percent, by definition you have the ability to pay off floating-rate debt any time you want to.

The final principle—really a kind of meta-principle or big picture principle—is that *the great majority of financial advisors*, even smart, dedicated, caring ones, are completely unaware of Strategic Debt Philosophy and Strategic Debt Practices, which means they *won't be aware that you may have a variety of superior options when it comes to purchasing expensive items.* You must find an advisor who understands and advocates the value of Strategic Debt for affluent individuals and families.

WHAT DO COMPANIES DO?

Like the other ideas we have discussed the goal is to eliminate the terms *good* or *bad* with respect to fixed- and floating-rate debt. Both have their advantages and disadvantages. Like everything in this book the relative merits of each should be considered based on your individual situation. Companies recognize this and often use a combination of both fixed- and floating-rate debt. You may be able to do the same!

Should Your Residence Be Treated Differently?

Recall that in Chapter 3 we discussed the fact that one's primary residence might deserve different treatment with regard to including it or not including it in your debt ratio calculations. Similarly, for some people, getting a fixed mortgage rate on their primary residence is an important emotionally rooted value that cannot, and should not, be disputed. They may feel that a fixed-rate mortgage decreases their risk and cost of financial distress.

Regardless of your views with respect to a primary residence, it is important to carefully analyze floating-rate debt and the concept of self-insuring when looking at financing second homes. If nothing else, this exercise should help shed light on the potential impact on your portfolio of a rising-rate environment.

Someone who is unaware of the concept of an ideal debt ratio, someone who hasn't thought about the fact that the financing around an item is 100 percent independent of the worth of that item, and someone who doesn't realize that amortization stinks and fixed rates often amount to an expensive and unnecessary insurance policy isn't going to be able to advise you as best as possible. So if you are working with an advisor who isn't familiar with all of these ideas, consider it your job to bring up these different ideas so that you end up with the best possible financing of whatever it is you want to purchase. And if your financial advisor or private banker is not open to understanding and exploring them, then you just may want to find yourself a new advisor.

A Better Way to Purchase a Vehicle (or Almost Anything Else)

Suppose Sam, who works as a senior associate attorney, has his eye on a lovely BMW convertible that will cost him about $75,000. Sam has had a good year and has just received a good bonus, his old car is about ready to give up the ghost, and he has always wanted a convertible.

Sam's first impulse is to go to the bank and get a 6 percent loan with a four-year amortization schedule, resulting in a monthly payment of about $1,761 a month. At the end of three years, he would still owe about $20,500 on the car. Let's consider, however, some other options that might be available to Sam. One thing he could do would be to use most of his after-tax bonus to pay down $35,000 on the vehicle, and then pay for the remainder of the price—$40,000—by writing a check against his ABLF. Assuming his cost for the line was 3 percent, Sam would be paying about $1,200 a year, or $100 a month, in interest ($40,000 × 3% = $1,200/12 = $100 per month), as opposed to roughly $1,761 a month. Plus, he would have no applications to fill out, no fees, no credit checks, and so on.

While comparing a $1,761 payment per month to a $100 payment per month isn't exactly apples-to-apples since the larger amount includes a principal payment, it is important to stress how much financial flexibility is implied by only having a $100 monthly payment. Remember that you likely don't even have to pay on a monthly basis if you don't want to! (Be sure to confirm your institution offers this level of flexibility on your specific ABLF). Because Sam has the ability to pay the ABLF off at any time, he is able to create this flexibility in his life and this reduces his likely risk and costs of financial distress.

Another option, though, would be for Sam to put that $40,000 from his bonus into his portfolio (potentially raising the total amount he can borrow on his ABLF) and pay for the entire thing, all $75,000, with a check written against his ABLF. At 3 percent this would cost him about $2,250 a year in interest, or roughly $188 a month. However, unlike with an amortizing loan, with most ABLFs, as long as he doesn't get close to his maximum draw, Sam wouldn't actually have to pay any of that $188 a month in interest or any of the principal until he was good and ready. If Sam continues to do well and his overall debt ratio remains in the desired range, say 20 to 30 percent, then it may not make sense for him to pay down the money used to purchase the car for a long time, if ever, a topic we'll return to in the Conclusion to this book. The key is that Sam—not the bank—would be in complete control of the payment schedule, and he would not have tied up any of his capital in a depreciating asset.

Is there another, even better possibility? Well, if Sam is able to take out a home equity line or loan, then that money would also potentially be tax deductible. So if he can get a home equity loan for the $75,000 at 3 percent, and he is roughly in the 33 percent tax bracket, then that money would effectively cost him 2 percent. That would amount to $125 interest owed on the money every month, with no amortization, no application fees, and as long as his overall debt ratio is in the ideal range, no need to rush to pay down the line. Compare that with the $1,761 a month it would have cost him had he gone to the bank (not to mention the loss of control he would have over timing of payments).

HOME EQUITY LINE OF CREDIT OR ABLF?

I often get asked, "Should I have a home equity line of credit or an ABLF?" The answer is that you should have both! There are advantages and disadvantages to each facility. A home equity line of credit (HELOC) is a great tool and the advantages are obvious (additional credit availability and potential tax deductibility—but be careful, as it is an add back for the alternative minimum tax). On the other hand, if you need to move, you may no longer have access to the line. Banks have also reduced and revoked lines in difficult times (right when people need them the most). For many high net worth individuals, a HELOC will provide some flexibility but will not be large enough to implement many of the ideas in this book.

These ideas apply equally well to many other types of assets. Suppose, for example, you are interested in investing money in a restaurant. Well, so-called restaurant loans, in a manner similar to boat loans, are for the most part very undesirable: expensive, short-term, low loan-to-value ratios, and inflexible. If you use your ABLF instead, you can get better rates, better terms, and not have to worry about exactly when you will be forced to repay the bulk of the loan.

Or suppose you want to buy a horse. If you buy a quality competitive horse, by the time you get done with all the gear that goes with it, it can easily cost you $20,000 to $50,000 or more. Most competitive riders only hold any given horse for three to four years. Well, what does horse financing look like? How many years do you amortize a horse over? If you use your ABLF to purchase the horse, and the horse costs $50,000, and you are paying a 3 percent rate, then that comes out to about $1,500 a year. Of course, the horse will ride up and down in

---

AN ABLF IS A TOOL TO USE FOR BETTER FINANCING OF . . .

- Cars (traditional, luxury, super luxury/exotic, race cars)
- Boats
- Planes
- Artwork
- Jewelry
- Antiques
- Start-up businesses
- Raw land
- Real estate
- Restaurants
- Existing business
- Private equity ventures/handling capital calls
- Mortgage alternative—especially in cases of bad or no credit
- Refinancing multiple types of existing debt (credit card, student loans, debt within existing insurance policies)
- Elder care bridge loan
- Disaster recovery
- Helping out family members (children, parents, incapacitated relatives)

value, but once again, the value of an item (including a fine animal) is independent of the financing in place around that animal.

This same sort of logic applies to everything from antique cars and investment-grade coins to Renaissance paintings and vacant land. If you qualify for an ABLF at a decent rate, paying for items by drawing on the ABLF gives you many advantages. (And if you haven't already put into place a home equity line or loan, in some situations that might be an even better option given the potentially tax-favored nature of such loans.)

Let's now expand the framework that's been considered for purchasing expensive items and apply a different solution—one that very few people know about—to what may be among the largest purchases you are likely to make, that is, a second home.

Purchasing a Second Home: Pluses and Minuses

In Chapter 3, when discussing how to determine your optimal debt ratio, we discussed at some length the question of whether your primary residence should be included in your optimal debt ratio. We concluded that for some people, there's no question that their primary residence should be free and clear—with no debt on it—as this is emotionally important to them. However, as a way to add desirable debt into your overall financial equation, the purchase of a second home may prove very promising.

Before considering how you might go about purchasing a second home, let's start by reviewing some of the disadvantages of owning a second home and whether you might want to just rent a vacation home instead. That is, before even beginning to look for a second home for vacation or investment or adding in good debt to the mix, you want to be well aware of the expenses and other factors typically associated with owning a second home. Let's go through these one by one.

Depreciation

To begin with, homes have multiple expenses associated with them that are often not fully factored into the cost of ownership and the likely rate of return on the property, starting with depreciation.

If you were to build a new house and leave it in the middle of a cornfield for 50 years, and then you came back and visited it, there'd be no part of the property that you would still be able to use. You'd essentially have to replace everything—the house would need a new roof, new windows, new carpeting, new appliances, new bathrooms, and so on. With a 50-year time horizon, this implies a 2 percent annual depreciation on the house just to maintain it and keep it exactly the same; if you assume a 30-year period, then that means approximately a 3 percent yearly depreciation cost.

It is important to apply this to the value of the building and not the land. So let's say that you have a lot worth $100,000 and you have a $1 million property on that lot for a total value of $1.1 million. In this example it is reasonable to assume that you will have somewhere between $20,000 and $30,000 a year of maintenance expenses just to keep the building in the same condition. Alternatively, if you have a $5 million property with $2 million of structure and $3 million of lot, then your depreciation may run closer to $60,000 per year (3% × $2 million). Separating the land value from the building value is particularly important in areas with high land values (coasts and cities) and less important where the land value is less than 30 percent of the value of the property.

Clearly these expenses won't be evenly distributed. With respect to new construction, the first two years tend to be expenses that are more related to finishing work versus maintenance. Years 3–10 tend to not have as much maintenance, but homeowners tend to underestimate the deferred maintenance that is building up. Years 10–20 tend to have a lot of expenses—most everything that plugs in, carpets, potentially the roof, and certainly the paint, and let's not forget that the entire decorating scheme will become outdated. Years 20+ tend to normalize in the 2–3 percent range. Normal may be a $10,000 expense one year and a $30,000 driveway the next, that is, normal won't be even on a yearly basis, but over a three-year period a total of 6–9 percent will most likely be the total cost that was reinvested into the property.

Do remember to factor in a homeowners' association fee or condo fee, if you have it; in effect it will typically cover a part of the depreciation because the association is keeping up certain areas such as the exterior of the property, the roof, and the common elements that you might otherwise be maintaining on your own if it was a single-family detached home.

Taxes and Operating Costs

Property taxes tend to run between 1 and 2 percent depending on where you live (although there are places where it is higher and places where it is lower).[4] You will also have operating expenses that could range from .5 to 2 percent or more, which includes everything from insurance to heating, gas, utilities, cleaning, lawn care, and so on. (Again, if you are in a condominium situation with a homeowner's association, they may cover some of these expenses, but then, of course, you also have the homeowner's association fee to consider.)[5]

Cost of Funds (direct or opportunity cost)

It is important to consider the actual cost of debt (the cost of debt after all tax implications) for the financing that you have in place vis-à-vis the *opportunity cost* of any equity that you have in the property. Perhaps it goes without saying, but any equity that you choose to tie up in a second home could be invested and, therefore, could return whatever the average return will be for the rest of your portfolio. Bottom line: There is a cost to using debt and a cost to using equity. Companies look at this through their weighted average cost of capital (WACC).

Up-Front Transaction Costs

Unlike the other expenses, this is not recurring but should be factored in as it is still significant. Closing costs, of course, range by area but are generally between 1 and 2 percent of the value of the property. These can include appraisal, inspection, title insurance, legal fees, and so on. Many markets now have mansion taxes and/or mortgage taxes on mortgages over a certain size that need to be factored in to the equation as well. Regardless of whether a property that you purchase is brand-new construction or a historic home, it is unlikely to be 100 percent perfect. If it is 97 percent perfect, you will have to put about 3 percent of the purchase price into the home to make it be just what you wanted. Typically this 3 percent is related to decorating/personal taste and adds little to the value of the property. Expenses associated with moving and furnishing can be considerable and may also factor in to a rent versus buy decision.

Liquidity (the ability to sell at a good price when you want or need to)

With respect to any real estate dealings, you should know that when you close on a property, unless you were very lucky, it is likely that you paid the highest price for that property at that point in time. If you wanted to turn around and resell the property immediately, not only would you typically have a roughly 5–6 percent real estate commission, but you would also most likely sell it for 2–3 percent less than you paid for it. In other words, one problem with residential real estate is that right after you buy it, if you want to turn around and sell it, you will take an approximate 7–9 percent hit, in addition to the roughly 4–8 percent in annual expenses.

But what about *appreciation* on second homes? Isn't real estate among the best investments you can make in the long run? Well, residential real estate certainly has the possibility of being an investment that can keep pace with inflation over time. Think about a home that your parents or grandparents lived in the 1950s or 1960s and what that house was later sold for in the 1980s or is worth today. Over long periods of time, it can appear that residential real estate has been a great inflation hedge.

However, this notion of real estate's increasing value over time can also be misleading. Unlike a stock or bond where you purchase the asset and have nominal tax consequences along the way (generally the only taxes due are on income or dividends that have been received, which is in effect a net reduction of the gross amount you have received along the way), you will pay property taxes (along with the above-outlined expenses) all the way along. Moreover, residential real estate does not generate income or pay dividends to the owner unless it is rented, which both changes the characteristics of what we are discussing and requires further injections of capital to maintain and manage the asset.

It can be tricky to determine a property's actual appreciation in value over time, in part because there's a distinct human tendency to deceive ourselves, and we all want to think we've done better than we've actually done. Consider the following example: If you buy a home for $500,000 and sell it for $1 million 10 years later, there is an appearance that you doubled your money or had an approximate annual return of 7.2 percent. However, if you paid a total of $60,000 in property taxes (factoring in any potential tax benefits) and invested $150,000 in the property for maintenance, upkeep, and remodeling, your actual basis is $710,000, which is what grew to $1 million over 10 years, a 3.5 percent rate of return (less the opportunity cost of the equity or any interest expenses).

With all of the above in mind, if you really have a desire to spend some time at a second home, for vacation or other purposes, the question then comes to this: Should you *rent or own*?[6] In a typical rental contract the owner of the property is responsible for all repairs, maintenance, taxes, and homeowners association fees, and obviously provides the property (meaning you have no debt or equity tied up in the property), which frees up the renter's capital. You are trading one fixed cost to replace several direct and indirect expenses.

Ultimately, the most important factor is *how many nights you are likely to be in a rental property a year.* In general the math works out roughly as follows.

Consider renting if:

- You are at a property less than 30 nights per year.
- And/or you are only at a property for a consecutive series of dates and not in and out throughout the year (e.g., winter or summer only).
- And/or you plan on being at that property for less than three years (too many transaction costs to recover in too short of a time).
- And/or you do *not* intend to rent the property (not renting effectively increases the cost).

Consider buying if:

- You intend to rent out the property.
- And/or you will be there more than 30 nights (especially if you will be there over 120 nights) per year.
- And/or you will be there throughout the year.
- And/or you believe there is a likelihood of appreciation at least equal to (or greater than) inflation.

MATH NOTE

Consider taking the total after-tax cost of all of the expenses mentioned earlier, subtract your appreciation assumption, and divide by the number of nights you will be there to get an estimated cost per night. This can be represented by the formula:

Estimated annual cost/number of nights you anticipate being there

Where the estimated annual cost = (appreciation + income) − (recurring expenses + (one-time costs/number of years in the property))

For example:

☺ **Appreciation and Income**

+ appreciation assumption
+ rental income (if any)
= approximate annual gain

☹ **Recurring expenses**

−2.5% depreciation
−1.25% property taxes
−1.5% operating expenses
−% after-tax cost of funds (ideally factoring in your WACC)
= recurring annual expenses

☹ **One-time costs:**

−__% transaction costs
−__% Liquidity costs
= one-time costs

Compare this figure to your rental alternatives. Rental income, appreciation, cost of funds, the number of nights you will be there, and your anticipated holding period are big drivers of the formula.

A detailed example of renting versus buying can be found in Appendix B.

100 Percent Financing: The No Down Payment Real Estate Purchase Option

Let's assume that you have decided that you do, in fact, want to purchase a second home. You can, of course, go the conventional route, and find the best possible mortgage through a bank or a mortgage broker. There is another option, however, whereby most major firms can offer you a 100 percent financing option against the value of a home. Basically, the firm will take a security interest in the home—like any bank or mortgage owner will do—as well as an interest in a pledge account that you will make with your existing assets at the firm, a pledge that covers the down payment on the home.

Here's what this looks like. Suppose you want to purchase a $1 million dollar residence with 100 percent financing along these lines. A traditional mortgage will typically be at about 70 percent for a second home at this dollar amount. Instead of putting down $300,000, you could do 100 percent financing—all as a first mortgage at the same terms as a traditional loan. To do this, in addition to having the property as collateral, the firm could also ask you to pledge, for example, 200 percent of the $300,000 down payment, or a $600,000 pledge account. (Note that you are *not* allowed to use the same assets that you may have pledged to get an ABLF and the exact pledge amount can and will vary by firm.)

With this kind of 100 percent financing, instead of coming up with a separate down payment—say, by selling $300,000 of assets—you are instead pledging assets that you already have invested with the company. Instead of disrupting your portfolio or finding some way to come up with enough liquid cash, you are able to cross-collateralize your existing portfolio, thereby making good use of your Indebted Strength of Increased Leverage to move into a mortgage (which may have tax-favored deductions) at an attractive rate.

Let's continue the math on this $1 million, 100 percent financed example. As discussed with fixed versus floating rates, if you own your primary house outright and your debt ratio is under 25 percent (with the mortgage), you might choose to get a mortgage that floats at a spread over LIBOR. These loans are available for around 2 percent in the current interest rate environment. After you figure in the tax deduction (if you are in the 33 percent tax bracket), you would effectively be paying about $1,100 per month (2% × (1 − .33) = 1.32%. 1.32% per year × $1 million = $13,200/12 = $1,100) while enjoying a million dollar home—and you didn't put any money down. Of course, there will still be the taxes, maintenance, and so on, as described earlier. But still this can give you a tremendous amount of flexibility as you go forward in life.

At this point nearly everybody asks two questions: What if the value of the property falls? And what if interest rates rise? This is why the foundation we have built is so important. As we learned, the value of the property is independent of the financing in place around the property. Its appreciation or depreciation is an independent event from the financing in place around that asset. With respect to interest rates, the movement of interest rates is covered under the fixed versus floating section in this chapter and in Chapter 5 on capturing the spread. If you maintain a debt ratio of 25 percent then by definition you have the ability to step in and *pay off the loan any time you do not like the strategy*. At the same time, it is imperative that you study how your portfolio is positioned for the risks of a rising rate environment.

HELPING OUT YOUR CHILDREN, PART 2

An ABLF was the first way to help your children but there is another way to help them as well. You should know that most firms also have a version of 100 percent financing that enables parents to do the same thing for their adult children.

Parents can pledge assets that will enable a child to avoid having to come up with a down payment. If the child wants to purchase a home for $300,000, he or she would need to come up with approximately a 20 percent down payment of $60,000. Alternatively, depending on the institution, the parents can pledge roughly $120,000 of assets. This pledge will enable the child to have a 100 percent loan with no PMI (private mortgage insurance), and the parents stay fully invested in their accounts in their investment strategy.

The parents are not cosigners and they are only at risk in the event that the child stops paying the loan. In essence, they are there as a backstop or additional collateral in the worst-case

(Continued)

scenario. The parents' assets continue to be invested, and whatever returns they generate go exclusively to the parents' account. The parents can typically continue to buy and sell investments, just as they normally would, as long as the assets they are buying and selling conform to ABLF requirements and they maintain the minimum amount required by the firm in the pledge account. This is a very powerful tool for families to discuss and consider (but read Appendixes B and C first!).

This can enable the purchase of a $300,000 property at, say, 4 percent fixed: $300,000 × 4% = $12,000 per year/12 = $1,000 per month. This $1,000 would be a tax deduction to the child. As you will see in the case studies and in Appendix B, additional savings from this strategy should not go to paying down the mortgage. It should go to building up cash, retirement plans, and liquid investments.

P.S.: The family should work together to determine if fixed or floating is a better decision. If you choose fixed remember that you are only trying to insure against the movement of rates during the time period the child anticipates owning the property. It can generally make sense for conversations to start around loans that are fixed for five to seven years (interest only) and adjust up or down from there.

Chapter 6: Summary and Checklist

This chapter considered better ways of buying expensive items, including everything from boats and cars to horses and jewelry to second homes or vacation homes. We began by considering how companies buy expensive items using a holistic and pragmatic approach that considers all of the available loan and financing options, including what the lowest long-term cost of debt to finance something will be.

We then reviewed four principles, including (1) the relationship between the type of financing you use to acquire an item and the value of that item (hint: *There is no relationship*, that is, they are completely independent); (2) the fact that amortization stinks and should be avoided whenever possible as required monthly payments, no matter what else is happening in your life, greatly limits your flexibility and can lead to or exacerbate financial distress; (3) the fact that purchasing anything with a loan with a fixed rate means you have paid a substantial premium for what is in effect an insurance policy that the interest rate won't rise; and (4) a kind of meta-principle or big picture principle that holds that the great majority of even smart and dedicated financial advisors are not aware of the value of Strategic Debt, and probably have not thought about these different sorts of financing options—which is why it is up to you to raise these possibilities.

We concluded by looking at a better way to purchase a vehicle or almost anything else through your ABLF or a home equity line or loan. We then considered the plusses and minuses, generally, of purchasing a second home, and then finally looked at what we've called the 100 percent financing option when it comes to buying a second home or vacation property, or helping your adult children get into a home.[7]

Checklist

❑ Can you see the value of financing the purchase of expensive items the way a company might do it, that is, holistically and pragmatically in the context of your overall balance sheet?

❑ Do each of the four principles discussed in this chapter make sense to you?

❑ Can you see how 100 percent financing using pledged assets might be extremely useful in certain situations?

Notes

1. Stephen A. Ross, Randolph Westerfield, and Jeffrey Jaffe, *Corporate Finance*, 10th ed. (New York: McGraw-Hill, 2013), Chapter 15. This is true with respect to corporate bonds. There are examples of certain asset-backed securities such as equipment trust certificates that railroads have used (among others) that either have direct amortization or a toggle feature that can trigger amortization. There also are mortgage-backed securities that contain an income stream that is comprised of both principal and interest payments. Many private company bank loans are subject to amortization terms. The fact that these loans and securities exist does not preclude the fact that publicly traded corporate debt is issued on an interest-only basis.

2. While no public traded companies issue bonds with built-in amortization, there are indeed amortizing bonds issued in the private equity markets. Also, corporations will establish sinking funds for their bonds where the money needed to repay the principal is put into escrow. However, the company still controls the cash and the ongoing payments they make on their debt will be interest only, that is, the only time you will receive a repayment of the principal is when the bond is called or matures. An individual can, of course, create a sinking fund as well.

3. When adopting this self-insuring perspective, keep in mind that when interest rates rise, the average return on fixed investments like bonds and even CDs may also tend to rise as well. Accordingly, depending on portfolio positioning, one may be better able to continue to afford this kind of self-insurance even if the cost of your debt rises over time. It should also be noted that there are multiple "spread products" that one can invest in that target a spread over floating rates, regardless of where those rates are in any economic cycle. Of course these funds may not be able to accomplish their objective. Sophisticated investors may also hedge against these risks or dramatic movements in interest rates with futures or options contracts.

4. "Median Effective Property Tax Rates by County, Ranked by Taxes as a Percentage of Household Income, 1 Year Average, 2010," The Tax Foundation, July 27, 2012. http://taxfoundation.org/article_ns/median-effective-property-tax-rates-county-ranked-taxes-percentage-household-income-1-year-average.

5. Yingchun Liu, "Home Operating Costs," HousingEconomics.com, National Association of Home Builders, February 8, 2005. http://www.nahb.org/generic.aspx?sectionID=734&genericContentID=35389&channelID=311.

6. Ross, Westerfield, and Jaffe, *Corporate Finance*, Section 21.9: Companies lease many assets.

7. The information in this chapter is to be considered in a holistic way as a part of the book and not to be considered on a stand-alone basis. This includes, but is not limited to, the discussion of risks of each of these ideas as well as all of the disclaimers throughout the book. The material is presented with a goal of encouraging thoughtful conversation and rigorous debate on the risks and potential benefits of the concepts between you and your advisors based on your unique situation, risk tolerance, and goals.

Chapter 7

Generating Tax-Efficient Income in Retirement or Divorce

Introduction: Three Goals (and Some Disclaimers)

The three main goals of this chapter are:

1. To illustrate how you can create tax-efficient (and potentially tax-free) income in retirement.[1]
2. To challenge and expand your understanding of taxes generally— and what to do about them.
3. To briefly indicate how these first two ideas can be applied, when possible, to optimizing divorce scenarios as well.

You can think of this chapter as presenting solutions to a gigantic problem, so it's not surprising that the ideas you'll find here are large and somewhat complex. Over time—and with a bit of luck—the big ideas found in this chapter will have their own book-length treatments, expanding on the ideas and scenarios found here and providing many more detailed examples. In the meantime, please consider this a big picture overview and know that every possible scenario cannot be covered here.

A quick caveat: Our tax code has nearly 4 million words and has gone through more than 5,000 changes since just 2001.[2] It is not possible for a book, let alone a chapter of a book, to fully cover all of the regulations or complexities within our tax system. The premise on which these ideas are based may change on a moment's notice. Further, these concepts may not apply to your individual situation. Accordingly, this section should in no way be construed as giving tax advice.

While there is risk in discussing these ideas in a constantly changing environment, there is risk in not presenting them as well. Many individuals take a complex code and reduce it to overly simplistic assumptions. As we will see, often these assumptions are wrong and accordingly lead people to make suboptimal decisions. The ultimate goal of this chapter, then, is to challenge some basic assumptions and raise more questions than answers. These questions may then serve as a jumping off point for discussions with your advisors.

An Opening Scenario for No Taxes in Retirement

Let's assume a scenario in which the following is true for you:

- You have no debt.
- You own your house outright.
- You have a $1 million liquid, after-tax, globally diversified portfolio that is fully eligible for an ABLF.
- You want—or need—$40,000 per year of income (which amounts to a 4 percent distribution rate vis-à-vis your $1 million dollar portfolio).

Given these facts, is there any reason why you would not simply take $3,333 a month—$40,000 divided by 12 months—in the form of a draw from an ABLF? Let's consider the tax consequences of implementing this strategy under current law:[3]

- *Zero income tax consequences*: There are no income tax consequences from borrowing money in this way. Funds from a loan come back to you tax free.
- *Zero estate tax consequences*: Under current law there would be no estate tax consequences.
- *Zero capital gains*: You have not sold anything. Significantly, the cost basis for the next generation steps up when you die.

Given the preceding scenario, the bottom line is that *you would pay zero in taxes on the draw you receive by implementing this strategy*. While your portfolio might generate some income in the form of dividends—dividends that could trigger taxes—the dividend stream and tax consequences of what you hold can in theory be controlled by your portfolio manager. For example, you could choose to own a portfolio of companies that do not pay dividends or you could own municipal bonds. Further, by integrating the ideas later in this chapter, even the portfolio income may be taxed at rates under 5 percent and as low as zero percent.

Some may try to position this idea as a "no tax retirement income strategy." Although conceptually there are similarities, technically this is not true as loan proceeds cannot be considered income. It is worth comparing and contrasting this approach with a traditional way of investing and how people approach and define "income."

Borrowing Versus Selling to Access Your Money

Many investors today use a strategy where they focus on "total return." This means that they do not just rely on the actual income (in the form of say, interest and dividends), but rather evaluate the income and the appreciation of the portfolio. An investor may, for example, target a 6 percent total rate of return. Perhaps their goal is that 4 percent of this comes, on average, from appreciation and perhaps 2 percent, on average, from income in the form of interest and dividends. If this investor wants a 4 percent income stream to cover their cost of living then their actual income (in the form of interest and dividends) of 2 percent would not be sufficient to accomplish their objective. Accordingly, this investor would have to sell 2 percent of their portfolio per year.

The net result in this example would be: 2 percent received as actual income + 2 percent liquidated as supplemental proceeds = 4 percent total received + 2 percent reinvested (or not liquidated).

Investors that take this approach know that they will *not* average a straight 6 percent return every year. Similar to the concepts expressed in Chapter 5, capturing the spread, total return investors are likely to have periods where their investment returns are below average and periods where they are above average. They measure the total return (income + appreciation − depreciation) over time relative to their goals. The phenomena of periods of over- and underperformance must be factored in to the overall financial plan.

Some readers will recognize that the concept of total return investing referred to is perhaps best reflected in The Prudent Management of Institutional Funds Act of 2006 which was designed to replace the Uniform Management of Institutional Funds Act of 1972 ("UMIFA"). Although written for institutional funds (such as trusts and endowments), there is a great deal of educational value in being familiar with these acts. According to the Uniform Law Commission, "UMIFA initiated the concept of total return expenditure of endowment assets for charitable program purposes, expressly permitting prudent expenditure of both appreciation and income."[4] A lot of the financial services industry has subsequently conformed to this standard in the advice that they deliver. Accordingly, *most advisors do not recommend that individuals seeking an income stream rely solely on the actual physical income from the portfolio* but rather take a total return approach to investing.

Under this style of total return investing, the traditional approach is to sell the balance needed to hit your return objective. In the example above, the investor wants 4 percent, the actual income is 2 percent and so accordingly they will have to sell 2 percent.

The benefit to selling is that you have liquidated the funds you need at that point in time. Assuming you keep the proceeds in cash then by doing so you no longer have market risk on that portion of your portfolio. The disadvantage of course is that you no longer have the funds invested—you sold them.

The reverse is true with borrowing. Instead of a sale, you now have an outstanding loan. Therefore, the disadvantage is that you are not only continuing to take market risk, but also you have the added cost of borrowing (and therefore interest rate risk as well). The advantage is that you still have the funds invested. As we further explore this idea we will see that this dilemma brings us right back to the potential risks and benefits of trying to capture the spread. If you capture a spread, this approach could add value. If you do not capture a spread, this approach will increase your risk and destroy value.

Make no mistake; there are multiple risks to the strategy of selling your assets as well. There is a risk of adverse tax consequences that can be triggered by the sale. Perhaps more importantly it is worth studying the risks associated with the fact that you no longer own the asset. If you sell then it is a mathematical proof that (1) you have a zero percent chance of participating in any potential upside on what you sold and (2) your future goals must be able to be accomplished off of a lower starting value. Intentionally reducing your investment base may be appropriate but the risks need to be compared to the benefits—and risks—of the alternative strategy of borrowing.

It is perhaps most important to note that this does not have to be an "all-or-nothing" approach. An investor could of course consider a hybrid method comprised of partial borrowing and partial liquidation. Keep this in mind as we move deeper into our understanding of taxes later in the chapter. The key is to be aware of your options, know the pros and cons of each and to evaluate based on your personal resources, goals, and objectives.

A Better Alternative to a Familiar Story

There are other products in the investment world that enable (and some encourage) you to do exactly the strategy just recommended. Although they position themselves as the only way to do this, the fact is, you can synthetically create that same story using an ABLF. Put differently, this isn't a made up story of how you can fund retirement in a tax-free manner using loans; instead, it is modified based on an existing story that is very popular.

There are multiple potential benefits to this approach that should be compared to the other alternatives including cost, liquidity, and investment flexibility. You could structure this portfolio so that the fees are very inexpensive. You could also structure it so that it is a very liquid strategy; that is, it is easy to get out. Generally, if at any time you don't like the way things are going with the ABLF-based option, you can simply pay off what you have drawn on the ABLF and move on in any direction that you prefer. The third benefit is that you have investment flexibility. Using the ABLF you can invest in virtually any publicly traded security (you may want to check to be sure the security you purchase is eligible to secure your ABLF). These benefits should be compared to alternative products that express your ability to take out money tax free in the form of a loan.

Tying It Back to Capturing the Spread

With the strategy that has been described here for funding your retirement needs, you retain full flexibility in terms of the securities in which you are investing. You can invest in most any publicly traded security (use caution as ineligible securities will be excluded from your loan availability calculation). However, the general problem with investing in some assets, such as equities, is that their returns are by their nature much more volatile. This raises many questions concerning the synthetic retirement strategy outlined earlier:

- What will the rate of return be on your portfolio?
- What will be your cost of debt?
- What will your rate of return look like over time? (How does it graph out?)
- What if we go through another 2008 Great Recession type of event, or even another Great Depression? That is, how sensitive will this portfolio be to volatility, and how do you protect against the downside?
- Will there be any tax consequences at all? What will be the impact of any dividends, and will you get a deduction from any interest expenses?

The big picture key here is that if your ABLF costs you 3 percent and your portfolio is averaging 6 percent, then you are successfully capturing the spread, which brings us right back to the importance of the ideas that were expressed in Chapter 5.

But what if interest rates rise? Clearly, this is a real risk. Importantly, rising interest rates can not only put downward pressure on bonds and

TWO ADVANCED EXERCISES AND A CAVEAT

1. SOMETHING TO MODEL—A CURVED DEBT RATIO OVER TIME

If on average you can outperform your cost of debt by 4 percent, and your return on assets exceeds your distribution rate on average by 2 percent, then generally your debt ratio will likely increase, cap out, and then over time it will gradually come down again.

2. PURPOSE OR NONPURPOSE ABLF

In implementing a strategy of borrowing to access your funds it is important that you visit with your advisors about whether your ABLF should be structured as a purpose or nonpurpose loan. As a part of this process you will want to see if your advisors classify any of your interest as tax deductible. If they do, it will be important to know if this expense may offset any of your other forms of income such as interest or dividend income. To keep the examples simple we will leave out this potential benefit in the scenarios as we move forward.

3. A CAVEAT

There are two main components of the idea of borrowing instead of liquidating to access your money: minimizing taxes and capturing the spread. By borrowing instead of liquidating assets to generate the needed cash flow stream in retirement you may save a lot in taxes, which in effect reduces your required distribution amount (how much you need to take from the portfolio). However, if minimizing taxes is what strikes you as the most interesting part then be sure you are armed with the right tax facts before taking the risk associated with the strategy. For some the tax savings may be more than you would estimate (as the end notes at the end of the chapter show) while for others it may be much less than you would estimate.

stocks, but they can also increase your borrowing costs—a triple threat that is discussed in more detail in Appendix C. Knowing that interest rates are low today and may—will probably!—change over time, it's useful to think in relative rather than absolute terms. Returning to our previous language from Chapter 5, it's useful to think about these issues in terms of the likely spread that will result.

Our objective here, then, has been to introduce these ideas rather than graph the many potential outcomes that follow from an in-depth analysis. Make sure you work with a qualified wealth management team to model these ideas with a particular emphasis on stress-testing for a range of outcomes in the portfolio, and make sure that the aggregate draw that you receive keeps you within your optimal debt ratio.

Revisiting Tax Issues

Many financial advisors and private bankers quickly—and rightly—say that they do not give tax advice. While they can't—and shouldn't—give you tax advice, they need to know the important and relevant facts relating to taxes so that you can (1) put into place the right investment plan and (2) have a strong basis for speaking with and receiving advice from your accountant. Moreover, your financial advisor has a tremendous ability to impact your tax situation in retirement by choosing how much comes out of qualified and nonqualified plans, how much is liquidated versus borrowed, and how much income is tax exempt versus tax qualified versus taxed at ordinary rates. To avoid poor or incorrect decisions, you, your financial advisor or private banker, and, of course, your accountant must get the tax facts straight. While a thorough discussion of taxation is far beyond the scope of this book, in this section I will review some of the most important and misunderstood facts about taxation.

Let's start with a simple question: Which is taxed at a higher rate, long-term capital gains or ordinary income? When I ask that question to financial professionals, 99 percent of the time the crowd roars back, "Ordinary income!" It turns out, however—as with nearly every other topic considered in this book—that it depends. You see, ordinary income is in fact often taxed at a much *lower* rate than long-term capital gains.

> Ordinary income is often taxed at a rate *lower* than long-term capital gains!

Mitt Romney got into trouble on this exact subject when he asserted in the 2012 election that 47 percent of Americans do not pay federal income taxes. According to ABC news,

> In 2011 . . . about 46 percent of the people who filed taxes, did not pay a penny in income taxes, according to an analysis of IRS data by the bipartisan Tax Policy Center. But that does not mean nearly half of America skirted their federal tax burden.

> Nearly two-thirds of the households that did not pay income tax in 2011 were on the hook for payroll taxes, a 4.2 percent tax that is automatically deducted from workers' paychecks to fund Social Security and Medicare.

> Only 18 percent of tax filers did not have to pay either income tax or payroll taxes.[5]

In retirement you are no longer collecting a paycheck, and thus you are not impacted by the payroll tax. Similarly, you would also not be paying any Medicare-related tax.[6] This implies, as will be explained shortly, that one of your goals is to have a certain minimum level of ordinary income—you want to be part of that 18 percent that didn't pay either income or payroll taxes!

As most of us are aware, and is illustrated in the preceding case, a family of four that makes $40,000 a year pays close to zero federal *income* tax. However, capital gains is currently set at a flat tax of 15 percent. (This is conceptually accurate but does not transcend all taxpayers. Importantly, this number can, and likely will, change over time.) The question then becomes, how much ordinary income can you have so that you will be taxed at a rate equal to or less than long-term capital gains?

To answer this, consider the difference between your marginal tax bracket and your effective tax bracket. Your marginal tax bracket is the stated rate at which you pay income taxes, but your effective tax bracket is the total tax paid, divided by your total adjusted gross income. Marginal tax rates will always be higher than your effective tax rate. Your effective tax rate, then, is where you actually fall in terms of your tax rate, that is, the total tax that you truly pay. Many deductions—including mortgage interest, charitable contributions, property taxes, medical expenses, and investment fees—reduce the amount of your ordinary income that is taxable. Therefore, you need to have ordinary income in the first place in order to maximize your benefits.

While detailed tax scenarios are beyond the scope of this book, I encourage you to validate the following scenario by working through a sample tax return using the information at www.irs.gov or with the help of your tax advisor and/or an online tax calculator such as those available at www.turbotax.com.

NOT TAX ADVICE BUT POINTING YOU IN THE DIRECTION OF TAX FACTS

A book like this cannot give you tax advice; put more directly, any tax advice that you act on must come from your tax advisors. It is important to keep in mind that there is a tremendous amount of debate around tax policy in the United States. Even by the time this book is published and available for purchase, tax reforms may be enacted into law that could challenge, modify, or completely change some of this chapter's underlying premises, suggestions, or facts. Again, that is why it is best to think of this chapter as providing a set of starting points—ideas to ponder and consider—rather than serving as a comprehensive guide.

Run the following scenario: Determine the tax implications for a 65-year-old retired couple—Mr. and Mrs. Webster—with $160,000 of total income broken down as follows:

- $80,000 IRA distribution
- $20,000 interest
- $20,000 dividends
- $20,000 Social Security
- $20,000 long-term capital gains from rebalancing

Please notice that outside of any required minimum distribution (RMD) and Social Security payments, with the help of their financial advisor or private banker, it is possible for the Websters to control the total amount of retirement income they receive (the amount of any IRA distribution, the amount of interest and dividends received, etc.).[7]

> Outside of an RMD, Social Security, and pension, your advisor is a driving force in determining your taxable income in retirement!

Their income stream is independent of their financial assets—just as the income statement is separate from the balance sheet for companies. It is related—and interconnected—but largely independent.

For example, the Websters could have a $2 million IRA and a $2 million investment account, and they could own their $1 million primary home outright and have a $1 million second home. Their total assets are $6 million. They could have a $500,000 mortgage on a second home for a total liability of $500,000. Their net worth, of course, would then be $5.5 million ($6 million assets − $500,000 in debt = $5.5 million). If they had $1 million in an index fund with a 2 percent dividend and $500,000 in municipal bonds and $500,000 in bonds with a 4 percent taxable income stream and took out $80,000 per year from their IRA, then they would look exactly like the preceding scenario.

Consider that the Websters also have the following expenses:

- $20,000 of charitable donations
- $20,000 of property taxes
- $10,000 of mortgage interest ($500,000 at 2 percent)
- $30,000 of professional/investment fees

Working with the aforementioned tools—and assuming the 2012 tax code is in effect—you'll be able to see that the Websters' total tax will be under $5,000, for an effective rate of about 2.7 percent. The Websters can therefore have $160,000 of income minus $5,000 of taxes, for a total of $155,000 of income after taxes. They could also consider borrowing from their ABLF an additional say $5,000 per month, creating roughly $18,000 per month of after-tax funds.[8]

ONLY $5,000 IN TAXES

Put differently, by utilizing the ideas and practices of Strategic Debt Philosophy as described in this book, the Websters—a retired couple worth $5.5 million—are able to spend roughly $216,000 per year after taxes ($18,000 per month) while paying approximately only $5,000 in taxes!

Notice that in this scenario the Websters are total return investors and that they are using a combination of income (interest dividends), liquidation (from the IRA), and borrowing (from the ABLF).

This raises a key question: Do the Websters want more capital gains or ordinary income? Using IRS Form 1040 (or your CPA or online calculator), try increasing their income by $100,000 to a total of $260,000 and you will see that their balance due becomes roughly $39,000, which happens to be about 15 percent of $260,000. You read that correctly—although the Websters are in the 28 percent bracket, they are paying an effective rate of 15 percent (and technically, including the AMT [alternative minimum tax] that they pay, they are still at the 15 percent effective rate).[9]

TAX MATH AND TAX QUESTIONS

I completely understand that 15 percent capital gains rate is less than the 28 percent marginal rate, I also understand that AMT is taxed at a rate higher than 15 percent. I am simply pointing out that the preceding scenario, which is comprised of $260,000 of income, is being taxed at an effective rate of 15 percent, which is nowhere close to 28 percent.

There are many aspects of the last scenario that are sub-optimal and they could take multiple steps to optimize their taxes. Clearly from these levels they have a preference toward capital gains and/or to defer income and/or to increase

(Continued)

deductions—perhaps with the use of additional debt. Once you get to this level you open up a series of questions for you and your advisors such as the following:

Basic questions:

- What is your effective tax rate?
- How much ordinary income is optimal for you? (Hint: The answer is not zero.)
- What is the crossover point between your preference for ordinary income and capital gains?
- What would the impact be of a $ _____ mortgage at __ percent? If rates rise to __ percent, how does that impact your taxes?
- How can a debt philosophy using a combination of an ABLF and mortgage(s) benefit you from a tax perspective?

Intermediate questions:

- What will be your sources of ordinary income in retirement?
- What exactly is generating this income and why?
- Can it be controlled?
- Are you making the right assumptions regarding the benefits of a Roth IRA? (Hint: Typically people do not; they overestimate the benefit and/or do the opposite of what they should do.)
- Are you making the right assumptions on how income from an annuity will be taxed? (Hint: Typically people do not; they underestimate the benefit of an ordinary income stream.)
- Do you understand when you want to increase ordinary income to benefit from deductions? Do you then understand how increasing income may impact a phase-out of other deductions that are beneficial?

(*Continued*)

TAX MATH AND TAX QUESTIONS (*Continued*)

Advanced questions for high wage earners:

- What would be the impact of placing $ ___ per year into your (deferred compensation/retirement plans)? Should I be deferring ($50,000/$250,000/$500,000)?
- How could an annuity complement a deferred compensation program?
- How can tax consequences be minimized through dollar cost averaging into a portfolio?
- What is the tax savings today versus the impact of it coming out as ordinary income in retirement? (This, of course, ties back to your sources of ordinary income in retirement.)
- The Alternative Minimum Tax makes the tax code more complex. Do you understand how to make this complexity work to your advantage?

My reading of the press (and our tax code) is that apparently income up to $250,000 is good, income over $250,000 is bad, income over $500,000 is really bad, and if you are making over $1 million, well, apparently some people think you don't deserve that. If that is the deck of cards we are dealt then you can play a strong hand using a combination of these strategies!

Once again, the bottom line here is that you need to sit down with your professional advisors and have them work together in a fully coordinated way to understand and implement these ideas and strategies. Have them run various scenarios and focus on the bottom line amount of taxes that will be due. While marginal tax rates are important to understand, it's at least equally important to understand the bottom line and your effective tax rate. Far too much attention is typically paid to marginal tax rates, and this leads individuals, families, and advisors to jump to the wrong conclusions about taxes and to

A TAXING QUESTION: UNPATRIOTIC?

Some of you may be concerned that the materials in this section of this chapter are somehow unpatriotic. Well, if you apply these and related strategic debt strategies and feel that your tax bill is too low, you are, of course, welcome to send in additional funds to the IRS. I am not—and have never been—an elected official, and so it is safe to say that I have had nothing to do with designing our tax code. It seems to me, therefore, that these ideas are in fact quite patriotic in the sense that it is not fair for some people to be aware of these ideas and strategies while others have no clue whatsoever as to what is possible along these lines. If bringing forth these ideas helps trigger a healthy and honest debate on tax policy, then as a nation we will all be the better for it.

make suboptimal decisions. Look, don't guess about the tax code—invest time and know the tax code.

From a wealth management and investment management perspective, the implications of correctly understanding taxes—along the lines of the Strategic Debt Philosophy and Practices discussed throughout this book—are huge. As an example, let's very briefly revisit a rising interest rate scenario. Let's assume you have a floating mortgage on your primary residence. If the interest rate is currently at 2 percent, and if the rate at some point in time goes up to 7 percent, the tax deduction would go up as well. Remember that mortgage interest (for now) is an off-the-top deduction and is not subject to the AMT (but is subject to size limitations). Once again, you always have to look at your after-tax cost of that debt. The higher your income and the more tax rates rise and the more interest rates rise, the greater will be your combined benefit from that loan. You can't look at the rate movement in and of itself, but instead you need to look at the after-tax cost of the loan with everything relevant taken into account.

In addition, as a general premise, you need to think about how you want to trigger income that is generated within your portfolios. As the Websters' case study showed, it can be very advantageous to draw on a line of credit or an ABLF over time versus liquidating portfolio assets to create a low-tax retirement situation.

WHAT ABOUT THE FUTURE?

The United States and countries around the world are engaged in a tax debate that is likely to continue for years—if not forever. Some proposals recommend increasing the capital gains rate, and/ or increasing the taxes on interest and dividends, and/or increasing ordinary income tax rates. Should that be the case then you will certainly want to dust off this book and revisit these strategies because the higher rates go, the more valuable they become.

There are so many different proposals that it isn't worth getting into exact detail at this time but suffice it to say that if, or when, higher rates occur, you should look for an updated volume with advanced strategies based on that environment.

I am already building 11-foot ladders for the 10-foot walls that could come our way.

Making Use of Strategic Debt Strategies and Practices in Divorce

Just as having zero debt is not the optimal, holistic, or most effective capital structure for someone who is retired, it also may not be the optimal capital structure for those involved in divorce situations. There are two parties to any divorce, and both may benefit by implementing the ideas of Strategic Debt Philosophy and Practices. All too often, divorce becomes a tug-of-war where the two parties are trying to divide one pie into several pieces, none of which seems big enough. But by applying Strategic Debt Philosophy and Practices, you can actually change—that is, increase—the size of the pie, leaving everyone involved better off.

Debt and divorce is complicated and represents a combination of the ideas in Chapters 4, 5, 6, and 7 coming together. The current combined balance sheet needs to be looked at with respect to how it is positioned relative to the optimal range of 15 percent to 35 percent. Overleveraged balance sheets (and those at the higher end of the range) may need to look at decreasing the total amount of outstanding debt to the target or lower end of the range as the cost and risk of distress has likely gone up for both parties. The strategic use of debt may also help those who are on the lower end of the range (or have no debt at all), making the pie bigger for both parties. In these cases debt may be able to create liquidity to resolve conflict over illiquid assets (such as closely held businesses, personal property, real estate), and it may enable both parties to better live the lifestyle they are accustomed to living.

WARNING—TOO MUCH MATH AHEAD!

The next discussion puts some detail around buying a house after divorce. Here is the bottom line: After divorce renting can make a lot of sense for the same reasons we discussed about second homes earlier and the renting versus buying math found in Appendix B. There are so many moving parts that I can't stress enough the importance of making conservative decisions and maintaining flexibility. I feel the more moving parts you have, the greater the value of flexibility.

If you do decide to buy then you should evaluate your options very, very carefully before paying cash for that property. Depending on your individual circumstances, a mortgage could be very beneficial, and there may be reasons why paying cash could be like shooting yourself in the foot.

If you fully understand the math and then decide to pay cash (under the premise of owning your primary home discussed in Chapter 3), then that is one thing, but please be sure you understand the strategic benefits of debt—including how it may minimize the tax consequences of alimony—before making that decision!

We are moving into advanced ideas, so feel free to skip to the chapter conclusion or follow along . . .

But what about taxes in divorce situations? It is terribly complex but certainly worth reading IRS Publication 504. Most people don't understand that the difference between alimony and child support is that alimony is treated as pretax money that is paid as taxable income to the recipient, while child support is considered after-tax money that the recipient receives tax free. Understanding the difference between these two types of treatment, especially in a progressive tax system such as ours, is essential. We often fall back on what things are generally called and then assume that certain types of money or payments must be used for that specific purpose. Of course, there could be reasons that alimony or child support may need to be established for their traditional intended purpose. However, in some cases, nothing could be further from the truth. Here we will focus only on the tax issue, which is one piece of a complex pie.

Ideally a divorce could be structured so that both parties have considerable deductions. In some cases (such as the Websters) this could include property taxes, a mortgage, charitable donations, and so on. An individual with a low tax burden and high deductions may be relatively indifferent to alimony and child support, up to a certain point. High wage earners, however, have a huge preference in favor of paying alimony because each dollar paid might create a tax deduction that could be worth over 40 percent when including state taxes (of course, the benefit might not be this high). Taken together and looked at holistically, this creates an opportunity to make the pie bigger.

Let's use the same scenario and same tools as the Websters, modified only slightly for the divorce. Let's assume that they are younger so they are not on Social Security. We'll say that they are both 45. They also have three children all under the age of 16. Let's then strike *IRA distribution* and replace it with *alimony*. You now have a divorced individual with $80,000 of alimony, $10,000 of interest, $10,000 of dividends, and $10,000 of long-term capital gains (in this example the last three components of income are half of what the Websters had as a joint couple). Assuming $10,000 of mortgage interest (perhaps they take over one house and the mortgage associated with it), $10,000 of charitable donations, $10,000 of property taxes, $15,000 of professional/investment fees (the mortgage interest being the same and the last three expenses being half of the Websters' example), the total tax due on the $110,000 of income would be about $5,000.[10]

For a high income individual, paying $80,000 of child support requires approximately $133,000 of ordinary income ($80,000/(1 − 40% tax rate) = $133,000). This means that on $133,000 of income the individual would be paying $53,000 to the government and $80,000 to his or her former spouse. As we saw in IRS Publication 504, child support is after-tax money for the payer that is tax free to the recipient. Accordingly, the individual would receive no tax deductions on the payment.

What could the person do instead? If the individual instead structured that money as alimony, the receiving spouse would not only receive the $80,000 with limited tax consequences as previously shown, but also the paying spouse would receive an $80,000 per year tax deduction. This deduction may be worth as much as $32,000 to the paying spouse. To be clear, the paying spouse has an expense of $133,000 in Scenario 1 and a net expense of $48,000 in Scenario 2. In both cases in this example, the receiving spouse receives approximately $80,000.

This example serves to illustrate that there is a possibility that a lot of white space may be able to be created that is *mutually* beneficial.

MARRIAGE PENALTY, INDEED![11]

A perverse by-product of our tax code is that a CPA may be able to illustrate a way that some married couples can increase their income by approximately $3,000 per month—after taxes—by being divorced. The example above is close to this and hasn't even gone through refinement!

With many of the tax proposals currently being considered by Congress, it is possible that such savings will go up. Should Congress maintain the same tax code but increase the tax rate on those making over x to, say, 50 percent or more and also limit their deductions, then from a financial perspective, might high income couples consider divorcing? One party could receive money as alimony, starting over in the progressive tax system. Potentially this arrangement might also expand the family's deductions.

(Continued)

MARRIAGE PENALTY, INDEED! (*Continued*)

You can imagine the conversation, "Honey, it's time to get divorced. Not because I don't love you anymore but because it makes more financial sense!"

I'm just here to report the facts. The couple can still be together in the eyes of their family, friends, and god—just not the government. There are risks and obstacles to this—some of which are covered in IRS Publication 504. In addition to the multiple obvious social challenges, there are disadvantages to this from a tax and legal perspective that are too vast to list. The IRS may disallow sham transactions, and they specifically address this notion in IRS Publication 17 by saying,

Divorce and remarriage: If you obtain a divorce for the sole purpose of filing tax returns as unmarried individuals, and at the time of divorce you intend to and do, in fact remarry each other in the next tax year, you and your spouse must file as married individuals in both years.

My point isn't at all that this is a recommended strategy but more an interesting cocktail conversation. At the end of the day it is up to you to decide which is crazier: these ideas or our roughly 4-million-word tax code and the incentives it may create.

The strategy can, of course, continue to be developed and is very iterative. For example, you could further increase alimony and then also increase deductions using a Strategic Debt Philosophy and make the pie even bigger. How could both sides potentially use an ABLF and or a mortgage and what are the potential benefits and risks?

Finally, it is essential to note that liquidity is often a big problem in divorce. Whether a closely held business is involved, or there are significant assets such as jewelry, luxury items, or collectibles that could be difficult to sell or split up, a shortage of liquid cash often arises. This is exactly where an ABLF can come into play to solve liquidity needs.

Once again, it is beyond our scope to run through all of the many potential divorce scenarios that are relevant here. The point of this chapter, obviously, has nothing to do with the actual tax figures that have been used here, but rather to focus on the Strategic Debt concept that can not only help a divorcing couple capture the spread but also help them be much more tax efficient generally.

Chapter 7: Summary and Checklist

Unlike last chapter, which focused on how to buy expensive items such as second homes or cars, this chapter focused on how to pay for two stages of life that often get the better of people, namely, retirement and divorce. The first goal of the chapter, then, was to show it is possible to access money tax-free by making use of a Strategic Debt Philosophy. Comparisons were made on the potential benefits and risks between a gradual liquidation strategy and a gradual borrowing strategy.

Issues of taxation were then revisited, including the differences between taxation of ordinary income and long-term capital gains. While ordinary income may occasionally be taxed at a higher rate, when looked at holistically, in a properly structured financial situation, ordinary income is in fact often taxed at a much *lower* rate than long-term capital gains. Much understanding can be gained by sitting down with a tax calculator and your advisors and looking at the entirety of your situation.

The chapter then made use of its look at taxation issues in presenting alternative strategies and options for optimizing divorce situations. When taking into account different taxation options and the willingness and ability to hold to each party's optimal debt ratio, it is possible to actually make the collective pie bigger, with both ex-husband and ex-wife (and any children) being better off than if things were not optimally structured.

Just like all of the ideas and suggestions in this book—but perhaps most importantly for this section—you should only move forward into actual implementation with the advice and council of your wealth

Many people take the tax code as a hand that is dealt to them that they cannot control. High net worth individuals and families with excellent professional advisors can use the complexity of the code to their advantage, and you should too.

management team, accountant, and attorney all working together. Then, you should regularly revisit these ideas and any actual implementations as your life, the market conditions, and the laws change and evolve, as they all certainly will. Like life itself, the application of the ideas in this book represents a moving target, so you have to stay nimble, seek the best advice you can find, and make sure that any solutions you are implementing are the right ones for you and your family.[12]

Checklist

❏ Were the big themes of the chapter—that both retirement and divorce can potentially be optimized by applying Strategic Debt Philosophy and Practices—understandable to you?

❏ Were the advantages of considering using a Strategic Debt Practice as part of a tax efficient retirement clear?

❏ Did the discussion of tax issues help clarify for you your own situation?

❏ Do you feel you have a good list of questions to frame the next visit with your tax, financial, and legal advisors?

❏ In situations of divorce can you see how making use of strategic debt strategies and practices in divorce can actually lead to a bigger pie where everyone involved is better off?

Notes

1. Tax laws are complex and subject to change. Tax information contained in this presentation is general and not exhaustive by nature. It is not intended or written to be used, and cannot be used, by any taxpayer for the purpose of avoiding U.S. federal tax laws. This material was not intended or written to be used for the purpose of avoiding tax penalties that may be imposed on the taxpayer. Individuals are encouraged to consult their tax and legal advisors (a) before establishing a retirement plan or account, and (b) regarding any potential tax, ERISA, and related consequences of any investments made under such plan or account. These materials and any statements contained herein should not be construed as tax or legal advice. Tax advice must come from your tax advisor.

2. Kelly Phillips Erb, "Tax Code Hits Nearly 4 Million Words, Taxpayer Advocate Calls It Too Complicated," *Forbes*, January 10, 2013. www.forbes.com/

sites/kellyphillipserb/2013/01/10/tax-code-hits-nearly-4-million-words-taxpayer-advocate-calls-it-too-complicated.

3. www.irs.gov.

4. http://uniformlaws.org/Act.aspx?title=Prudent%20Management%20of%20Institutional%20Funds%20Act.

5. http://abcnews.go.com/Politics/OTUS/mitt-romneys-47-percent-pay-income-taxes/story?id=17263629.

6. This is true with respect to payroll/income related Medicare taxes. The Affordable Care Act will trigger Medicare taxes on certain other types of income, particularly investment income for earners in certain brackets. www.healthcare.gov/law/full/index.html.

7. Stephen A. Ross, Randolph Westerfield, and Jeffrey Jaffe, *Corporate Finance*, 10th ed. (New York: McGraw-Hill, 2013). Chapter 19 addresses this subject in detail.

8. These figures come from the TurboTax calculator at www.turbotax.com. This is also available as an iPad application. Using TaxCaster 2012 with the following inputs: married, filing jointly, both age 65, $20,000 of interest, $20,000 of qualified dividends, $20,000 of long-term capital gains, $80,000 of IRA distribution, and $20,000 of Social Security benefits. Total income of $160,000 will show in the estimator as $157,000 for reasons outside of the scope of this note. Although this individual is in the 25 percent bracket, this is NOT their effective rate. Before applying the rest of the case, pause and notice that taxes due are $21,866. Continuing through the example on expenses: $10,000 in mortgage interest payments, $20,000 in real estate taxes, $20,000 in donations, $30,000 as an employee business expense (TurboTax does not have a line for advisory fees; check with your tax advisors as to your ability to deduct these fees and if placing this expense on this line represents an accurate estimate for your situation). The net result is actually $4,285 which was rounded up to $5,000 in the example. $4,285/160,000 is an effective rate of 2.7 percent.

   You can also go to www.irs.gov, search for Form 1040, and you can access the form and instructions to build scenarios, sample returns, and confirm these figures.

9. These figures come from the TurboTax calculator at www.turbotax.com. Using TaxCaster 2012 with the following inputs: married, filing jointly, both age 65, $20,000 of interest, $20,000 of qualified dividends, $20,000 of long-term capital gains, $180,000 of IRA distribution, and $20,000 of Social Security benefits. Total income of $260,000 will show in the estimator as $257,000 for reasons outside of the scope of this note. For expenses: $10,000 in mortgage interest payments, $20,000 in real estate taxes, $20,000 in donations,

$30,000 as an employee business expense (TurboTax does not have a line for advisory fees; check with your tax advisors as to your ability to deduct these fees and if placing this expense on this line represents an accurate estimate for your situation). The net result is actually $39,150 (which is comprised of $31,695 of taxes + $7,455 in AMT for a total tax of $39,150). You can also go to www.irs.gov, search for Form 1040, and you can access the form and instructions to build scenarios, sample returns, and confirm these figures.

Notice that the monthly after-tax income is $260,000 − $39,150 = $220,850. This is $18,404 per month. In the first scenario the Websters created $160,000 − $4,285 = $155,715/12 = $12,976 in after-tax income. The scenario went on to discuss the fact that they could take an additional $5,000 per month from their ABLF to create $18,000 per month (technically $17,976). If we round, in both scenarios the Websters are receiving approximately $18,000 per month in after-tax income. Accordingly, the benefit of the ABLF draw from a tax perspective can be estimated to be $39,150 − $4,285 = $34,865 per year. This is surprising because one could easily incorrectly guess that the maximum benefit of a $5,000 per month draw could be estimated by taking $60,000 × your effective rate. Notice that $60,000 × 28 percent = $16,800 yet the actual benefit of the strategy was almost twice that amount. This should reinforce a simple point: don't guess with taxes. Work with your CPA and other advisors, do the math and figure it out.

10. These figures come from the TurboTax calculator at www.turbotax.com. Using TaxCaster 2012 with the following inputs: single, 45, Head of Household, three dependents under 16, $10,000 of interest, $10,000 of qualified dividends, $10,000 of long-term capital gains, $80,000 of alimony. Total income of $110,000. For expenses: $10,000 in mortgage interest payments, $10,000 in real estate taxes, $10,000 in donations, $15,000 as an employee business expense (TurboTax does not have a line for advisory fees; check with your tax advisors as to your ability to deduct these fees and if placing this expense on this line represents an accurate estimate for your situation). The net result is actually $4,492 which was rounded up to $5,000. It is interesting to see that if you drop out interest, dividends, and capital gains and keep the deductions the same, the taxes due falls to zero.

11. The Internal Revenue Service, *Publication 17: Your Federal Income Tax*, 2012; www.irs.gov/publications/p17/ch02.html#en_US_2012_publink10001 70739.

Laura Saunders, "Wedding-Bell Blues," *Wall Street Journal*, weekend ed., June 8, 2013, B9. "For two-earner couples, marriage often means owing more in taxes every year—and this year's new provisions are raising the penalty. Here's what you need to know."

The case studies presented are for educational and illustrative purposes only and do not indicate future performance. Past performance is no guarantee of future results. Investment results may vary. Investing is risky. The investment strategies and products and services presented are not appropriate for every investor. Individual clients should review with their financial advisors the terms and conditions and risks involved with specific products or services. Neither the information provided nor any opinion expressed constitutes a solicitation for the purchase or sale of any security. All of the returns are hypothetical and not intended to demonstrate the performance of any specific security, product, or investment strategy.

12. The information in this chapter is to be considered in a holistic way as a part of the book and not to be considered on a stand-alone basis. This includes, but is not limited to, the discussion of risks of each of these ideas as well as all of the disclaimers throughout the book. The material is presented with a goal of encouraging thoughtful conversation and rigorous debate on the risks and potential benefits of the concepts between you and your advisors based on your unique situation, risk tolerance, and goals.

Chapter 8

Conclusion: What This Book Is Really About

When you have a sufficient amount of wealth,[1] having some of the right kind of debt—the smart kind of debt, the well-thought-through kind of debt—in your personal financial ecosystem is not only a good idea, in many cases, it's a great idea. The right kind of debt—what we've also throughout called Strategic Debt—gives you and your family more liquidity, more flexibility, more leverage, and more of an ability to survive whatever might happen in the future, including natural disasters, a death in the family, a career loss, and so on. Put differently, the right kind of debt can be absolutely invaluable to you and your family, and this book has aimed to explain at least the beginnings of how and why this is so, and how you can best take advantage of Strategic Debt.

But does *taking on debt when* you don't *have to* ever really make sense? Absolutely! (In fact, as we'll show later in this chapter, sometimes taking on more debt is the *only* thing that makes sense.) Here's the real key: This book is not about buying what you cannot afford, or living a lifestyle (including during retirement or divorce) that is beyond your means. Instead, this book is really about three things:

1. How to proactively prepare for potential disasters of all kinds by putting in place an ABLF.
2. How to increase your wealth and, therefore, the amount you can afford in the long-run by capturing the spread.
3. How to optimize what you can already afford by showing you the best way to pay for things, especially expensive items.

What We Hope You Have Taken Away

Ultimately, the goal of pulling together all of the information that constitutes Strategic Debt Philosophy and Strategic Debt Practices was to *challenge conventional wisdom and to encourage you to have an open mind and consider what might be optimal in your own case*. For starters, the very notion that wealthy individuals and families have something called an optimal debt ratio will be taken by many to be heretical. Why, just read the popular financial books, and they all say that you should get rid of all of your debt as soon as possible.

But those books and authors, respectfully yet bluntly, are not applying the rigorous thoughts of a CFO to their personal balance sheet. They often approach things atomistically, not holistically; they completely miss the fact that companies of all kinds choose to have the right kind of debt on purpose because it strengthens them from the inside out; and they obviously haven't thought through the potential benefits of having an ABLF in place. The notion of Indebted Strengths is completely foreign, and they apparently have never considered how having the right kind of debt can provide Increased Flexibility, Liquidity, Leverage, and Survivability. Needless to say, the idea of capturing the spread, which is a golden key that may radically upgrade the long-term wealth outlook for some of the readers of this book, is never even approached by these authors because it seems too dangerous and unorthodox. Of course, there are some kinds of debt that you simply shouldn't have, including, for example, ordinary credit card debt with high rates and bad terms, but we can't be so simple to say that debt is good or bad. Debt needs to be looked at within the context of your overall financial picture.

We hope, then, that you will think of having an optimal debt ratio as being an integrated part of your holistic financial plan. We also hope that when somebody approaches you with atomistic financing (car loans, boat loans, horse loans, etc.), you have just a twinge of anxiety and are filled with enough doubt that you call your financial advisor or private banker to see if there is a better way. And finally, we sincerely hope that we have conveyed to you the criticality of having an ABLF in place, not just to optimize the way you can finance the purchase of cars, boats, horses, raw land, restaurants, start-up businesses, and so on,

BEHAVIORAL FINANCE 101

The ideas that have been expressed throughout this book assume that you are willing to think like a CFO: intelligent, rational, and willing to make optimal choices. They assume, for example, that you are choosing between paying down debt and adding to your portfolio. They do not assume that you are choosing between paying down debt and buying a Ferrari. There is a growing body of work studying behavioral economics that shows that people are not in fact the rational robots that a text such as this assumes them to be.[2]

Many individuals have a very difficult time saving money. Moreover, many people simply cannot handle the discipline that managing a Strategic Debt Philosophy requires. There is a risk that some people who are driven by acquiring things will throw out the optimal part of this book and will use the ideas and strategies found here to justify purchases that they should not be making and debt that they should not be taking on. If you fall into this camp, then regardless of your net worth, the ideas in the mainstream media of eliminating debt, opting for short amortization schedules, and paying things off is perhaps the best advice that you will ever get.

but also—and no doubt more importantly—to proactively protect your family from disaster. Once again, when you need substantial amounts of liquid cash now, nothing beats being able to write a check from a proactively established account at a reasonable interest rate.

Further, we hope that you now know that there is much more to having a proper debt structure than assessing the interest rate you are paying on any debt that you already have. The interest rate on debt is no doubt a key component, but never underestimate the value of flexibility and how, for example, debt that has an amortization schedule attached to it automatically reduces such flexibility. Moreover, when life-changing circumstances come up for you or your family—divorce, retirement, the need to make an elder care bridge loan or to finance a child's education—we hope you are now aware that there may be different and unequivocally better options for paying for these needs.

Hopefully, then, you will strike the words *good* or *bad* from your vocabulary with respect to any of the following situations or circumstances:

- Paying down your debt or having debt.
- Paying off your mortgage or not paying off your mortgage.
- Having debt in retirement or taking on even *more* debt in retirement.
- Having debt after divorce or taking on even *more* debt after divorce.
- Having debt when you die versus passing on a clean slate to your heirs.
- Having fixed-rate versus floating-rate debt.
- Renting or buying a primary or secondary residence or vacation home.

In each and every one of these situations, there are multiple pros and cons, and in each of them, debt is neither inherently good nor bad. Each of these situations involves many considerations, and depending on those considerations, debt can either be potentially useful and beneficial or potentially costly and dangerous. Yes, you will have to sort through what, exactly, taking on debt means in any of these situations, and you will almost certainly need the help of an open-minded, progressive, and competent financial advisor or private banker to do so. Going against the commonly held perspective that all debt is bad takes a lot of guts, but it can also produce tremendous short- and long-term rewards for you and your family.

Strategic Debt as a Financial Engine over the Decades

Applying the ideas found in this book to your own financial life—especially if you take a decades-long perspective—is where things get particularly exciting. Nobody knows what the rate of return on your investments will be, and nobody knows what your future earnings and savings will look like. Still, it is useful to imagine and consider what one family's financial situation might look like over time if they embrace an optimal debt ratio. Don't get too caught up on the details of the scenarios here. Asset and home values can of course go down as well. Instead, just think of this as a story of one family and what might happen over time, and pay attention to some of the surprising dynamics involving wealth, debt, and optimal debt ratios. (We'll expand upon these sometimes surprising and paradoxical dynamics in the next section.)

In Table 8.1 we see the situation of a family who will be called the Young Accumulators. Here, their debt ratio is a bit high, at 40 percent, but debt ratios are often a bit high when a family is just starting out.

Embracing the ideas and strategies found in this book, Table 8.2 illustrates their balance sheet 10 years later after the family does the following:

- They never pay down their mortgage.
- They have all of their savings go into their investment portfolio.
- They take out a larger mortgage when they move into a bigger home.
- They have a higher absolute debt, but a *falling* debt ratio (since they have more assets too).
- They have access to an ABLF but don't use it yet, as there is no need and their debt ratio is still a sliver high (although within the 15–35 percent ideal debt ratio zone from Chapter 3).

Now, moving on to Year 20, Table 8.3 shows what happened with this family since Year 10 after the following events:

Table 8.1   Year 1 Balance Sheet

Year 1

Assets		Liabilities
Real estate	$ 500,000	$400,000
Investments	500,000	—
Total	1,000,000	$400,000
Net worth	$ 600,000	**40% debt ratio**

Table 8.2   Year 10 Balance Sheet

Year 10

Assets		Liabilities
Real estate	$1,000,000	$800,000
Investments	1,400,000	—
Total	2,400,000	$800,000
Net worth	$1,600,000	**33% debt ratio**

Table 8.3   Year 20 Balance Sheet

Year 20

Assets		Liabilities
Real estate		
Home 1	$1,200,000	$ 800,000
Home 2	800,000	600,000
Investments	3,500,000	—
Total	5,500,000	$1,400,000
Net worth	$4,100,000	**25% debt ratio**

- Their main house appreciates a bit, and they make no mortgage debt repayment on it.
- They decide to get a vacation home, as the family is at a great point in life to use it, and they take out a mortgage on this second house.

- They are not yet using—have not yet drawn upon—their ABLF, as no need has arisen.

Note that even having taken on a total of $1,400,000 of mortgage debt, they were able to bring their debt ratio *down* to the ideal 25 percent.

Next, between Year 20 and Year 30, a number of things happen for this family:

- Their main house appreciates a bit more.
- They upgrade their second home.
- They enter their Power Savings Years, building up their portfolio but not paying down their mortgage debt.
- They begin making use of their ABLF, and realize, with retirement beginning to approach, that they may be able to make even further use of their ABLF in retirement when the time comes (see Chapter 7).
- If the markets move up, and their investment portfolio appreciates, they may decide to pay down on their ABLF as they enter into retirement.

Significantly, as Table 8.4 illustrates, although the family's total liabilities in Year 30 are now $2,750,000 (as opposed to $1,400,000 in Year 20), their total assets are now $11,000,000 (as opposed to $5,500,000 in Year 20), leaving them with an ideal debt ratio of 25 percent (just like in Year 20).

Let's fast-forward once more 10 years to Table 8.5 where we see what happens in Year 40. In between Years 30 and 40, then, here is what happens with this family:

- They sell one house and downsize into a condo.
- Their retirement income comes in part from their ABLF and in part from trimming their investment portfolio.
- Their portfolio grows a little, but not a lot as these were expensive years for living, that is, the Go Years of traveling the world, helping family members, having two houses, and so on.

Finally, let's fast-forward 10 years one last time, to Year 50, as per Table 8.6.

Table 8.4 Year 30 Balance Sheet

Year 30

Assets		Liabilities
Real estate		
Home 1	$ 1,500,000	$1,000,000
Home 2	1,500,000	1,000,000
Investments	8,000,000	750,000
Total	11,000,000	$2,750,000
Net worth	$ 8,250,000	**25% debt ratio**

Table 8.5 Year 40 Balance Sheet

Year 40

Assets		Liabilities
Real estate		
Home 1	$ 1,500,000	$1,000,000
Home 2	500,000	500,000
Investments	10,500,000	1,625,000
Total	12,500,000	$3,125,000
Net worth	$ 9,375,000	**25% debt ratio**

Table 8.6 Year 50 Balance Sheet

Year 50

Assets		Liabilities
Real estate		
Home 1	$ 1,000,000	$ 800,000
Home 2		
Investments	12,750,000	2,650,000
Total	13,750,000	$3,450,000
Net worth	$10,300,000	**25% debt ratio**

The years between Year 40 and Year 50 aren't nearly as expensive since there is less travel and fewer expenses after the family downsizes its homes. In fact, they move to the independent living side of an elder care facility. Although the facility costs $10,000–$15,000 per month, they were previously spending $20,000 or more a month during their "Go Years." The annual cost of the elder care facility, then, is less than what they were spending on trips, cars, houses, family member needs, and so on, just a few years earlier.

The final upshot is that at Year 50, nearer the end of their days, while the family has greater liabilities than ever before ($3,450,000 in Year 50 versus $3,125,000 in Year 40), that is, greater *debt* than ever before, they also have a larger total portfolio than ever before ($13,750,000 in Year 50 versus $12,500,000 in Year 40) and a greater net worth than ever before ($10,300,000 in Year 50 versus $9,375,000 in Year 40). Put differently, as the summary Table 8.7 shows, by embracing Strategic Debt Philosophy and Practices—such as not paying down debt but instead investing money that would have been used to pay down debt into their investment portfolio where they successfully captured the spread—this family not only lowers its debt ratio over the decades until they reach and maintain an ideal debt ratio, but they live the life they want to while increasing their investment portfolio and net worth, leaving plenty of money for the next generation—or for charitable and legacy intentions—when the time finally comes.

Ask yourself, then, whether it's a problem that this family's total liabilities—their total debt—rises decade after decade. Atomistically perceived, that might be seen as a major problem. But holistically

Table 8.7   Summary Balance Sheet over Time

Year	Total Portfolio	Total Assets	Total Liabilities	Net Worth	Debt Ratio
1	$ 500,000	$ 1,000,000	$ 400,000	$ 600,000	40%
10	1,400,000	2,400,000	800,000	1,600,000	33%
20	3,500,000	5,500,000	1,400,000	4,100,000	25%
30	8,000,000	11,000,000	2,750,000	8,250,000	25%
40	10,500,000	12,500,000	3,125,000	9,375,000	25%
50	$12,750,000	$13,750,000	$3,450,000	$10,300,000	25%

contextualized—that is, given the context that their total assets, total investment portfolio, and total net worth have all risen even more—then their increasing liabilities can be seen in the correct light. Not only, then, is the ever-increasing amount of their total liabilities—their total debt—not a problem, it is an essential part of their success and the very economic engine that made it possible for everything else to go up so much over time.

Paradoxes of Plenty: Some Surprises in Maintaining an Ideal Debt Ratio

Let's look at just one more family's financial situation in order to help draw out some of the paradoxes and surprises that emerge from success-fully adopting strategic debt practices on a long-term basis. In Table 8.8, the Johnsons have a net worth of $3,750,000, with mortgages on two homes and an investment portfolio with an associated ABLF that has a $250,000 draw on it. Their debt ratio is at 25 percent, which we have defined in Chapter 3 as being at the optimal level.

Assume that the Johnsons' houses grow in value at a 2 percent pace and that their investment portfolio grows at 6 percent. In the next year, Year 2, Table 8.9 shows what their situation would look like.

The first thing to notice about Year 2 is that the Johnsons' debt ratio has declined from 25 percent to 24 percent (actually, 23.85

Table 8.8   Debt Ratio Paradox Year 1

Year 1

Assets		Liabilities
Real estate		
Home 1	$ 750,000	$ 500,000
Home 2	750,000	500,000
Investments	3,500,000	250,000
Total	5,000,000	$1,250,000
Net worth	$3,750,000	**25% debt ratio**

Table 8.9   Debt Ratio Paradox Year 2

Year 2		
Assets		**Liabilities**
Real estate		
Home 1	$ 765,000	$ 500,000
Home 2	765,000	500,000
Investments	3,710,000	250,000
Total	5,240,000	$1,250,000
Net worth	$3,990,000	**24% debt ratio**

percent), even though they did not pay down any debt. Let's assume that the Johnsons are still working and saving toward retirement. If they are saving, then by definition they have enough funds to cover their lifestyle. Let's also assume that they are happy with the life that they have and are living. How can they maintain an optimal debt ratio of 25 percent?

Well, not only would the Johnsons need to *not* pay down any debt, they would actually need to take on *more* debt to get things back to the 25 percent optimal debt ratio. But how can they take on more debt without acquiring more items (which we just stated they don't need, since they are already happy with the life they are living)? Well, they could choose to not pay the interest on their ABLF. As shown in Table 8.10, at a 4 percent interest rate, this would increase their loan facility from $250,000 to $260,000 over the year ($250,000 × 4% = $10,000 increase).

But still, this would just take their ratio up from 23.85 percent to 24.05 percent, which would still leave them in a suboptimal situation (with optimal defined as 25 percent). To get their debt ratio back to the ideal 25 percent, they would have to draw on their ABLF— in excess of the associated interest cost—an additional $65,000. Since their living expenses are covered, they would have to draw from their ABLF—almost $5,500 per month—to pay for trips, taxes, credit card bills, miscellaneous expenses, and so on. The $5,500 that they would

Table 8.10   Debt Ratio Paradox Year 2 without Paying Interest

Year 2

Assets		Liabilities
Real estate		
Home 1	$ 765,000	$ 500,000
Home 2	765,000	500,000
Investments	3,710,000	260,000
Total	5,240,000	$1,260,000
Net worth	$3,980,000	**24.05% debt ratio**

have been spending on those expenses now becomes savings and can be directed to their portfolio on a monthly basis! This is shown in Table 8.11.

Yes, this implies not only will the Johnsons not pay down their debt, but instead, they actually will want to increase their total amount of debt over time to keep at or near the 25 percent ideal debt ratio. Who else does this? Well, companies do exactly this.[3] If you think back to Chapter 1 and the second tenet—Explore Thinking and Acting Like a Company—we stated something then that is worth

Table 8.11   Debt Ratio Paradox Year 2 without Paying Interest and Increasing Debt

Year 2

Assets		Liabilities
Real estate		
Home 1	$ 765,000	$ 500,000
Home 2	765,000	500,000
Investments	3,775,000	325,000
Total	5,305,000	$1,325,000
Net worth	$3,980,000	**25% debt ratio**

repeating now: By and large, most companies have a debt ratio within a very close range of what they had 30 years ago, even though they have larger total assets and net worth. This means that they have had to regularly increase their total debt in order to maintain the same debt ratio. Finding ways of purposefully increasing one's desirable or strategic debt may seem counterintuitive, but it is often the best course to follow according to Strategic Debt Philosophy and Practices.

Interestingly, a kind of paradox emerges when you begin to successfully apply Strategic Debt Philosophy and Practices to a wealthy family's financial situation over time, especially if you set your goal on a specific optimal debt ratio, such as the 25 percent ratio we have been using throughout this book. (While on the one hand we don't want to have the ideal debt ratio tail wag the long-term financial dog, it does give us a good pole star to guide things by.) Simply put, if a family gets to the point—we'll call it the breakthrough point—where they are successfully capturing the spread (see Chapter 5), then drawing on their ABLF (or their home equity line of credit) more and more to take on more desirable debt may become necessary. But that means that all the money that might have otherwise been used to pay down debt goes into their portfolio, which means that their total portfolio, assets, and net worth will keep rising . . . which means that they have to put even more money on their ABLF draw!

It is essential to understand that this is based on the premise that the money that would have gone to pay down debt is instead going into a portfolio. It is not going to additional consumption. Similar to the notion of a positive feedback loop or the famed three-body problem in astrophysics, one's ideal debt ratio becomes harder and harder to achieve as one keeps successfully capturing the spread. This means that not only might such a family never pay down a dime on their home mortgage, but they might have to take on additional debt to keep their debt ratio near the ideal range. This also means that this family may end up never paying down any money they use from their ABLF to buy a car, or expensive jewelry, or whatever else they purchase using the methods described in Chapter 6. So yes, if you have saved sufficient assets, are capturing the spread, and are hitting the breakthrough zone, you can buy a $75,000 car and never pay a dime on it. In fact, when you reach that point, buying that car is one of the only ways that you could possibly maintain an optimal debt ratio! (Before you get too excited, see the important notes that follow.) Similarly, property taxes can be paid by drawing on one's ABLF, with the money that would have gone to the state instead going into one's investment portfolio, where it may grow at a greater rate than the cost of the ABLF debt.

It makes some people uncomfortable to think of dying with debt and passing debt on to the next generation members of their family. But once again, if that debt was necessary and useful in accumulating a greater net worth—if that debt is seen holistically in the context of its value in creating wealth—then there is really no problem here. Yes, debt will be passed on to the next generation perhaps, but more than enough wealth to cover that debt will also have been passed on (assuming proper tax-aware estate planning has been done).

IS DEBT REALLY A BAD DEAL IN INHERITANCE?

Imagine that you inherited a successful publicly traded company—every single share of it—so now you own it all. In owning all of the company, you would naturally also own, and be responsible for, all of its debts. You wouldn't say, "Oh man, I'm in a terrible situation! Look at all the debt I just inherited!"

Investing in the Future: A Cautionary Reminder

Clearly the preceding scenarios in this chapter hypothetically assume positive returns on average and over long periods of time. It is almost certain that investors will have periods of negative returns, periods where they are not capturing the spread. During those periods the opposite phenomena occurs where your debt ratio is rising. How do you manage this risk?

This becomes perhaps the most interesting conversation with your advisors because your debt ratio and the amount of debt you have could actually be used as a tool that you could vary within a range, depending on global economic conditions. During good times you may choose to step in and pay down some debt—lowering your debt ratio. During tough times you may then allow it to drift back toward optimal.

There is risk to letting it drift back up. Bad times can be more severe and enduring than many people think. You need to not only hedge these risks but also think closely—and proactively—about your debt ranges. What is your tolerance zone? At what point do you step in and pay down? How much would you pay down? How will you prevent what could become an unfortunate spiral? You should enter the strategy with an exit plan if things go wrong.

Once again, as detailed in Appendix C, "No Guarantees: Limiting the Risks of Investing in a Crazy World," your financial plan and, more to the point, your investment strategy must be prepared for an uncertain future. For example, your investment strategy should be positioned to recognize that it is very unlikely that the next 30 years can or will look anything like the past 30 years. Given that risk and reward are always tied together, make sure you are well aware that all investment strategies involve risk.

You, along with your financial advisor, should carefully consider what happens if the United States ends up looking like Japan over the past 20 years and their significant deflation. Or what if we end up looking like Argentina when they went through devaluation, then inflation, then hyperinflation? Or what about if we end up looking like Greece in the 2007–2012 period, England in the 1950s and 1960s, or France in the 1920s? How would each of these historical shock periods impact your investment plans, your long-term wealth, and your debt ratio? How would they impact your ability to capture the spread?

A critically important question, then, is whether you are properly proactively prepared, and properly hedged, for a wide range of outcomes. For example, are you sufficiently prepared to face the worst-case financial stress scenarios that might befall you and your family? At the very least, harkening back to the notion of the one thing you must consider, make sure you have an ABLF in place to help absorb, defray, and reroute the worst possible financial shocks that you and your family might experience. And make sure you are receiving the proper professional guidance—financial and otherwise—to help you plan for the future.

A Final Thought

A book such as this one cannot possibly cover everything of importance or relevance related to Strategic Debt Philosophy and Practices and the value of debt. Instead, my goal has been to give you some powerful ideas—ideas that quite purposefully run counter to the bulk of mainstream advice to get out of and stay out of all debt forever perpetuated by popular authors and inspire you to work with qualified professionals who can help you implement these concepts for the long-term well-being of you and your family.

By bringing these ideas together and presenting them to you, I hope to have put you on the path to truly realizing the potential of the value of debt in the optimal management of both sides of your balance sheet. May these ideas help you—in tandem with excellent professional financial advice—to maximize your wealth, minimize unnecessary taxes, and be well prepared for any crisis. Good luck, good health, and good investing to you![4]

Chapter 8 Summary: A Recap of the Book's Significant Lessons

- It is essential to know that this book is not about buying things you cannot afford. It is about better ways to finance and pay for the things that you can afford.
- Remember the five tenets of Strategic Debt Philosophy:
  1. Adopt a Holistic (Comprehensive)—Not Atomistic—Approach
  2. Explore Thinking and Acting Like a Company
     - Virtually every company of any size chooses a holistic approach to its balance sheet that embraces having both assets and debts.

- If you are a CFO of a public company and you haven't focused on your optimal debt ratio, do you know what you would be? That's right: You'd be fired.
- If companies are willing, able, and deeply committed to embracing Strategic Debt Philosophy and Practice, then you, as a natural, real, live person or head of a family, should also be willing to at least explore these ideas as well.
- 100 percent of all debt issued by publicly traded American corporations is issued on an interest-only basis.

3. Understand Limitations on Commonly Held Views of Personal Debt
- The real problem is the lack of education that almost everyone has about the use of Strategic Debt.

4. Set Your Sights on an Optimal Personal Debt Ratio
- Setting your sights on achieving that ideal ratio makes it far more likely that you will achieve it.

5. Stay Open-Minded, Ask Questions, and Verify What Works
- While financial distress itself cannot easily or usually be directly moderated, the likely impact, costs, and duration of financial distress can in many cases be addressed with the ideas and practices found in this book.
- There are four key qualities or Indebted Strengths that flow from the strategic use of debt:
  1. Increased Liquidity—having more ready access to liquid funds or cash.
  2. Increased Flexibility—more options for addressing the direct and indirect costs of financial distress and for moderating the level of impact.
  3. Increased Leverage—in good times, you have the ability to enhance and accelerate the accumulation of wealth.
  4. Increased Survivability—a diminished likelihood that real survival issues, to your way of life, or to life itself, will arise.
- If you do nothing else that this book suggests, find out if you qualify for an ABLF and do the paperwork necessary to put it into place before the funds are needed.
- Your debt-to-asset ratio = total debt/total assets
  - You are better served by being conservative and overstating the value of your liabilities.

- You are better off being conservative by understating your assets in the formula.
- Your rate of return on paying down debt is exactly equal to your after-tax cost of that debt.
- If you choose *not* to set up an ABLF, you may be increasing the likelihood that you will experience substantial financial distress.
  - If I were the president or CEO of a company and my CFO chose to not set up a line of credit and then a need arose, what would I do? I would fire him or her!
  - The same concept applies to your need for a line of credit for your family.
  - Many ABLFs are not used at any given point in time, but most are used at some point in time.
- If you feel confident that on average you can capture the spread then it may be worth exploring a Strategic Debt Philosophy and pursuing an optimal debt ratio. If you don't feel you can capture the spread you should consider paying off your debt.
  - Are there any investments, anywhere in the world, that you feel are highly likely to outperform the actual cost you are paying for your debt?
  - Understand that there will be time periods where you will "capture a negative spread"; periods where your investments will underperform your cost of debt.
  - Know that at any given point in time there will likely be (and according to some theories should be) assets that are underperforming your cost of debt. A strategy of capturing the spread should not be measured on an asset-by-asset basis over the short term.
  - *All things equal, a lower-volatility portfolio with debt may be better than a high-volatility portfolio with no debt.*
- There may be better ways to finance the expensive items you want and the lifestyle you need.
  - Always take a holistic look at your balance sheet.
  - There are often far better ways to purchase expensive items by making use of Strategic Debt Philosophy and Practices.
  - The value of an asset is 100 percent independent of the financing in place around that asset.

- The value you will receive upon selling an asset has nothing to do with whether or not that asset has a loan against it.
- You cannot change your net worth through financing.
- There are often far better ways to generate income for retirement or to structure divorce situations so that everyone is better off.
- The next 30 years cannot be like the past 30 years. Be prepared for a wide range of outcomes. The wider the range, the greater the increase in the risk and the potential reward of these strategies.
- *Most importantly: Stay open-minded, ask questions, and verify what works before taking action!*

Notes

1. The introduction states that the book was initially written for Accredited Investors; specifically those with at least $1 million in net worth excluding the value of their primary residence. You should discuss with your advisors whether or not these ideas are appropriate for you. Appendix B specifically addresses what those who are young and getting started, or who otherwise do not have this amount available, can do to begin taking advantage of the book's ideas, practices, and strategies.

2. Ziv Bodie, Alex Kane, and Alan Marcus, *Investments*, 9th ed. (New York: McGraw-Hill, 2011), Section 12.1, The Behavioral Critique in Investments.

3. www.federalreserve.gov/releases/z1/20110609/z1r-3.pdf.

   The case studies presented are for educational and illustrative purposes only and do not indicate future performance. Past performance is no guarantee of future results. Investment results may vary. Investing is risky. The investment strategies and products and services presented are not appropriate for every investor. Individual clients should review with their financial advisors the terms and conditions and risks involved with specific products or services. Neither the information provided nor any opinion expressed constitutes a solicitation for the purchase or sale of any security. All of the returns are hypothetical and not intended to demonstrate the performance of any specific security, product, or investment strategy. It is not the intention to have somebody go from no debt to a significant amount of debt in a short period of time. This action may not only be prohibited, but also there are significant risks to doing so that are discussed throughout the book in detail.

4. The information in this chapter is to be considered in a holistic way as a part of the book and not to be considered on a stand-alone basis. This includes, but is not limited to, the discussion of risks of each of these ideas as well as all of the disclaimers throughout the book. The material is presented with a goal of encouraging thoughtful conversation and rigorous debate on the risks and potential benefits of the concepts between you and your advisors based on your unique situation, risk tolerance, and goals.

Part 4

APPENDIXES

Men who wish to know about the world must learn about it in its particular details.

—*Heraclitus*

Appendix A

The Varieties of Debt

I t's important to gain a general understanding of the different types of debt that are out there and available to you. While this is less of a specific Strategic Debt Practice or application and more of a meta-practice or big picture practice, it is nonetheless very important, because it relates to and underlies all of the other practices. For example, the answer to whether to pay down a certain type of debt often depends on which kind of debt it is, and while achieving and maintaining an ideal debt ratio is very important, once again, you don't want to make that happen by taking on the wrong kind of debt.

To this end, Table A.1 lists the major types of debt that you as an individual or family are likely to have access to, along with a number of characteristics of that debt.

The far left column on the chart lists the different types of debt, and then for each type of debt the following characteristics are considered:

- *Favorable Interest Rates?*—Are the rates associated with this kind of debt usually good ones?

- *Tax Deductible?*—Debt that comes from a loan where the interest is tax deductible is very desirable. Depending on your tax bracket, the real cost of such a loan can be substantially less than the nominal interest rate you are paying. You will want to be sure you understand limits to deductions and if the deductions are an add back for the alternative minimum tax.

- *Amortization?*—A loan that has built-in amortization is something you should avoid whenever possible. Amortization means you will have an inflexible, minimum monthly payment, and so this works in the opposite direction of the Indebted Strength of Increased Flexibility. Whenever possible, avoid amortization.

- *Secured?*—A loan that is secured is in some ways less desirable, because it means you are pledging assets, such as portfolio investments or real estate, in order to get the loan. However, it is the "secured" part of a secured debt that enables the loan to take place in the first place and typically makes it available at a better rate than an unsecured alternative. It's good to remember, however, that you ultimately do have something at risk with a secured loan.

- *Fixed or Variable?*—While some people prefer the security of knowing that the interest rate on their debt cannot increase, what you are actually doing is purchasing a kind of insurance against rates rising later on. Unfortunately, insurance is sometimes expensive, so you may be paying more than you might really need to for the assurance that rates will not rise. Also, if you have a variable loan and rates do rise, keep in mind that your ability to earn interest on your investments may have risen as well.

The higher in the chart you find a particular type of debt, the more generally desirable that type of debt is. One type of debt that has not yet been considered is 100 percent real estate financing, which involves a pledge against portfolio assets as described in detail in Chapter 6. Both a regular mortgage and this 100 percent real estate financing are at the top of the chart because they may come with favorable interest rates and may be tax deductible. Next comes the ABLF. A home equity loan or line can also be a desirable form of debt in that it is tax deductible within limits.

Table A.1 Types of Debt and Characteristics

Type of Debt	Favorable Interest Rates?	Tax Deductible?	Amortization?	Secured?	Fixed or Variable?
Regular Mortgage	Yes	Yes, within limits	Depends	Yes	Either
100% Real Estate Financing	Yes	Yes, within limits	Depends	Yes	Either
Assets-Based Loan Facility (ABLF)[1]	Yes	See tax advisor	Not Typically	Yes	Typically variable but fixed available
Home Equity Line or Loan	Yes	Yes within limits	Not Typically	Yes	Either
Conventional Bank Loan (e.g., for a car)	Sometimes	No	Typically	Yes	Either
Unsecured Personal Line of Credit	No	No	Not Typically	No/personal guarantee	Typically variable
Student Loan	Yes, but varies	No	Typically	No	Typically Fixed
Credit Card Debt	No	No	Yes	No	Either, but even fixed cards typically have variable features

We then move down to conventional bank loans for expensive purchases such as cars, boats, and other luxury items. While such loans can have favorable teaser rates, they are not tax deductible and are usually both amortizable and secured. The devil is in the details with such loans, and they have to be looked at carefully. Next down are student loans, which usually but not always have good interest rates and are amortized.

The final type of debt, which should for the most part be fully avoided, is credit card debt. Although many credit card companies will offer low teaser rates, they count on the fact that sooner or later you will be late on or miss a payment, whereupon the rate skyrockets. Some people try to play a kind of game where they take on new credit card debt at very low rates and then shuffle that debt around with yet more credit card debt later on before the rates go up, but even if you don't miss a payment and pay off the balance before the rate rises, this practice will wreak havoc with your credit score and is just not worth it.[2]

Notes

1. See important notes in Appendix C on purpose and nonpurpose loans.

2. The information in this appendix is to be considered in a holistic way as a part of the book and not to be considered on a stand-alone basis. This includes, but is not limited to, the discussion of risks of each of these ideas as well as all of the disclaimers throughout the book. The material is presented with a goal of encouraging thoughtful conversation and rigorous debate on the risks and potential benefits of the concepts between you and your advisors based on your unique situation, risk tolerance, and goals.

Appendix B

Strategic Debt Practice for the Young and Those with Limited Assets*

R ight at the beginning of the introduction it is stated that Strategic Debt ideas and practices are *not* for everybody, and that, indeed, there are three prerequisites to making best use of this book:

---

*Past performance is no guarantee of future results. Investment results may vary. Investing is risky. The investment strategies and products and services presented are not appropriate for every investor. Individual clients should review with their financial advisors the terms and conditions and risks involved with specific products or services. Neither the information provided nor any opinion expressed constitutes a solicitation for the purchase or sale of any security. All of the returns are hypothetical and not intended to demonstrate the performance of any specific security, product, or investment strategy. It is not the intention to have somebody go from no debt to a significant amount of debt in a short period of time. This action may not only be prohibited, but also there are significant risks to doing so that are discussed throughout this book in detail.

1. Having an open mind.
2. Working closely with a progressive, holistic, open-minded financial advisor or private banker.
3. Having sufficient liquid, investible assets.

This appendix focuses on the third of these requirements, which is not yet having sufficient liquid investible assets to implement these ideas. Of course, the younger a person or married couple is, the less likely he, she, or they are to meet this requirement, and it is not surprising that few people or couples under 40 years of age, and far fewer under 30, qualify.

However, just because you are young and do not yet have the kind of necessary initial wealth—or just because you are older and have not yet put together the kind of additional wealth that will enable you to take advantage of the ideas and practices in this book—doesn't mean there might not be a great deal of value for you in these pages. To help you "get there," that is, to the place where you can start making use of the ideas in this book, here are Eight Guidelines—think of them as Rules of Thumb—that you may find both useful and very valuable in the long run:

1. Now you are in the Accumulation Phase
2. Beware of ongoing credit card debt
3. Keep enough liquid cash reserves on hand
4. Maximize your retirement-related investment opportunities
5. Focus on accumulating investment assets
6. Deprioritize paying down your mortgage
7. Consider renting instead of owning
8. Lower assets may be okay for an ABLF

First Guideline: Now You're in the Accumulation Phase

Whatever your age or current status, *think of yourself as now being in the Accumulation Phase* that will get you to the level of investable assets that will enable you to best use the ideas and practices found here. That is, assume that you *will* get to the place where you *can* make use of these ideas, and then do what it takes to get there.

Second Guideline: Beware of Ongoing Credit Card Debt

As you have no doubt heard from many sources, and as has already been discussed in Appendix A, *ongoing credit card debt is virtually always bad debt,* and you should do what you can to avoid it and to then pay it off as soon as possible. Credit card debt will be at a high interest rate that will go higher if you miss a payment; credit card debt has no tax advantages; credit card debt requires a monthly payment, thereby limiting your flexibility; and with regard to any ideas about wealth amplification by capturing the spread as discussed in Chapter 5, it is very difficult to get a greater return on any money you borrow on credit cards than the cost of the money.

However, *it is good to have some credit cards* because using them and paying them off fully each month will improve your credit score, which is important for getting mortgages, business loans, and so on. Also, while it's good for emergency and logistical purposes to have a large line of credit available on at least one credit card, you should never draw more than 50 percent of your available credit on any one card because that may substantially harm your credit score.

Third Guideline: Keep Enough Liquid Cash Reserves on Hand

Just like you don't want the oil in your car's engine to ever get to too low, you never want your liquid cash level to get too low. Every individual or family, then, should have a three- to six-month liquid cash reserve on hand—or instantly accessible—for emergencies. So if you spend a total of about $5,000 a month on average—and that should include all your spending, from housing to food to clothing to transportation to entertainment—then you should have a cash reserve available of between $15,000 and $30,000.

STRIVE FOR A PERFECT CREDIT SCORE

Perfect can be a stretch but at a minimum you should target a score over 800. Consider reading Al Bingham's book *The Road to 850: Proven Strategies for Increasing Your Credit Score*. Here are some steps to accomplishing this goal:

1. Use credit but use it responsibly.
2. Never draw more than 50 percent of your available credit.
3. Pay your bills on time and in full monthly.
4. Don't have a lot of cards—one or two primary cards and two or three store cards.
5. Use the same card for a long time—don't switch a lot.
6. Consider using a credit monitoring service.

Some people think of this as an Oh, Shoot fund. Whatever happens—whether you are being forced to leave a job or are choosing to quit, whether you get an urge to suddenly travel and visit friends or family, or whether there is a sudden emergency or opportunity that can only be addressed with real cash—you can say, "Oh, Shoot, I'm going to go ahead and do what needs to be done." Of course, unlike the inexhaustible guns we see in the movies and on television, you are limited to the number of money bullets you have to shoot, so make sure you *only* use your Oh, Shoot fund when it is absolutely necessary to do so.

In addition to a three- to six-month cash reserve, you should also have cash on hand (or short-term CDs) for any expenses you will have in

BE PREPARED TO LOSE YOUR JOB!

Always assume that the likely scenario is that you will lose your job at some point in your career (or as an economist might say, a job loss should be considered an endogenous—not exogenous—shock). I can't stress enough the importance for people of all ages—but especially for those in their 20s and 30s—of building up a healthy cash cushion and a solid Plan B.

the next 24 months. This could include expenses such as those related to education costs, major home repairs, vehicle repairs, and so on. The risk return trade-off over a 24-month period is too low to justify the risk.

Fourth Guideline: Maximize Your Retirement-Related Investment Opportunities

Once you have a cash reserve, make sure you are maximizing your potential contributions to any retirement plan you qualify for, especially if it is a retirement plan with an employee match, such as a 401(k). If you are eligible for an IRA or an SEP, it is generally a good idea to maximize your yearly contributions to these as well. Be sure you read Appendix C with respect to asset allocation and risks in the world. Like they say in baseball, aim for singles—don't swing for home runs, and do not take excessive risk. Any portfolio trading you do will most likely be a function of rebalancing to return to your desired asset allocation.

Fifth Guideline: Focus on Accumulating Investment Assets

Since it requires a minimum amount of liquid assets to be able to take maximum advantage of the ideas found in this book, after making sure you have a cash reserve on hand and have maximized your retirement investments, you should start in earnest to build up your tax-unencumbered investment assets. Regular small investments (such as what's called dollar cost averaging, where you put in the same amount into an investment fund every month) can get you to where you want to be sooner than you think.

Sixth Guideline: Deprioritize Paying Down Your Mortgage

As stated in Appendix A and elsewhere throughout this book, given the generally low rates and tax-advantaged status of mortgage debt, don't

BUILD UP LIQUID, AFTER-TAX INVESTMENTS

As expressed over and over in this book, too many young people value paying off debt versus the value of a liquid after-tax investment portfolio. Always remember what was discussed earlier in the book:

- The value of an asset is independent of what you owe on that asset.
- Amortization stinks (it increases your risk and cost of financial distress, reduces savings, and ties up capital in fixed assets).
- By paying down debt, your rate of return is exactly equal to your after-tax cost of that debt.

Note: Amortization may be very appropriate for those who do not have the discipline to handle the risks and responsibility associated with interest-only debt. Interest-only debt is risky, and the premise is that you are saving the difference, not spending it!

be in a rush to pay down the principal of your mortgage. It's generally better to build up your liquid cash reserves, optimize your retirement investments, and then start accumulating investment assets than it is to pay down your mortgage. For example, if you are 55 years old and have $250,000, you likely have a problem, because you probably won't be able to generate enough of an income stream from that amount. In this instance, there's no question that it would be far more desirable to build up your investment portfolio than it would be to pay down your mortgage debt.

Seventh Guideline: Consider Renting instead of Owning

If you are not yet a homeowner, and especially if you are young, think twice before rushing out to purchase a house, condo, or apartment. Often, people want to own a home just so they can feel that they own something of significance or they aren't throwing their money away on rent. However, unless you are going to stay in a home at least three years—and ideally five to seven years or more—it generally doesn't pencil out. Young people tend to move around quite a lot. They also tend to overvalue the benefits to ownership and undervalue the flexibility that renting provides.

With home ownership there are multiple risks. Clearly there is price risk. If you buy a $400,000 house and it goes down in value by 10 percent, you just lost $40,000, which is likely to be a considerable percentage of your net worth. In addition to price risk there are up-front transactions costs, there's a risk that something major can go wrong with the home (like needing a new roof), and there will certainly be ongoing maintenance, which some studies indicate ends up being about 3 percent of the value of the structure (excluding the land) on an annual basis in the long run. When you want to sell the home, there will be additional transactions costs—such as the 6 percent realtor fee—that will make it hard for you to come out ahead.

One of the greatest disadvantages to ownership is that it reduces your flexibility. Once you are in a property it is difficult to move to another property because your equity is tied up in a house. If you get a bridge loan to facilitate the purchase of another property, then you are increasing your risk and cost of financial distress as you have increased your outstanding debt and therefore your debt ratio. This lack of flexibility can impact your career; it can impact your love life.

Let's look at two examples of short-term home ownership, a Lucky One and an Unlucky One.

Example 1: The Lucky One

- Purchase price: $500,000
- Costs in decorating the place, getting it set up, and closing costs: $15,000
- Annual maintenance: $10,000
- Sales price: $600,000 three years later
- 6 percent commission and expenses upon sale: $36,000

The lucky individual spent $500,000 + 15,000 + $30,000 (three years of maintenance) + $36,000 commission = $581,000, and received

$600,000. His net gain was actually $19,000. But wait: He also had mortgage, homeowners association fee, insurance, and property tax expenses. He also had the expense of having had his equity tied up in the house (sometimes called the opportunity cost of capital). These expenses could easily have totaled 6 percent per year less perhaps a 2 percent tax benefit for a net cost of 4 percent or $20,000 per year. I would suggest that the total cost was $20,000 × 3 = 60,000 − $19,000 profit = $41,000 total cost or roughly $1,138 per month. Said differently, even with the gain they are neutral compared to having paid rent of $1,138 per month.

Example 2: The Unlucky One

- Purchase price: $500,0000
- Costs in decorating the place, getting it set up, and closing costs: $15,000
- Annual maintenance: $20,000 (the unlucky individual hit some bad luck and a series of major repairs had to be done)
- Sales price: $450,000 three years later
- Commission and expenses upon sale of 6 percent = $27,000

The unlucky individual spent $500,000 + 15,000 + $60,000 (three years of maintenance) + $27,000 = $602,000, and received $450,000. He lost $152,000, plus he had mortgage, homeowners association fee, insurance, and property tax expenses. With the same $60,000 in expenses, this ownership experience cost about $210,000 or $5,833 per month. Can this individual easily move for a job or a loved one? What are the indirect costs of this situation?

Although in a certain sense you are paying a premium for renting, and you are not getting a mortgage deduction, the benefits have to be weighed against the costs. Home ownership can prove a trap that can actually increase the likelihood that you will experience financial distress at a greater impact level, with higher direct and indirect costs, and for a longer duration. (See Chapter 2 for a description of financial distress, the costs of financial distress, and so on.)

RENT OR BUY?

Eliminate the terms *good* and *bad* with respect to most everything in your life, but especially with respect to renting versus owning. When I am teaching I often use examples from major publications that compare a house for sale for $4 million or for rent for $12,000 per month. I love it when I can get both numbers!

- Would you rent or buy?
- What are your assumptions in your decision?
- What is the implied cost of capital?
- Is the person paying $12,000 throwing away their money in rent?
- What is the flexibility of the renter versus the owner?

Eighth Guideline: Lower Assets May Be Okay for an ABLF

The amount of investible assets needed to use at least one of the ideas in this book—the assets-based portfolio loan—may be substantially less than you imagine. For example, if you have $200,000 of qualifying investible assets, and you put an ABLF in place with a maximum loan of $100,000, that kind of cushion— the ability to access that kind of liquid cash in an emergency—could be tremendously useful. No matter what, it is important for you to have access to some type of a line of credit. This could be a home equity line of credit, credit card, or an ABLF; there are benefits to having all three![1]

Notes

1. The information in this appendix is to be considered in a holistic way as a part of the book and not to be considered on a stand-alone basis. This includes, but is not limited to, the discussion of risks of each of these ideas as well as all of the disclaimers throughout the book. The material is presented with a goal of encouraging thoughtful conversation and rigorous debate on the risks and potential benefits of the concepts between you and your advisors based on your unique situation, risk tolerance, and goals.

Appendix C

No Guarantees: Limiting the Risks of Investing in a Crazy World

In any book on investments and finances, there will inevitably be a number of legal disclaimers along the lines of "Past performance is no indication of future performance" and "There are no guarantees that any particular investments recommended in this book will do well." Such statements are quite true and are meant to provide fair warning and to protect both the investor and his or her financial advisor (and the firm the advisor works for) from unreasonable expectations. As a starting point, then, keep in mind that when it comes to investing and performance, there never were (never will be and never can be) any ultimate guarantees.

Also, as was made clear from the beginning, this book is not—and was never meant to be—a detailed implementation manual or how-to book, with regard to the wise use of Strategic Debt and all of the ideas and practices associated with it. Instead, think of this book as a starting place for new ideas and ways of looking at things that you should *then review with your advisors*. For even though there are no guarantees in the bigger sense, the chances of you making the right short- and long-term moves for you and your family go up dramatically if you are working with a competent, honest, and well-intentioned financial advisor or private banker.

Whoever you work with, there are a number of fundamental concepts concerning risk that both you (and your family) and your advisor should be aware of. Here, then, we will very quickly review the nature of risk; we will then describe the historical landscape we find ourselves in today and where we are heading (previously discussed in an abbreviated fashion in Chapter 5), and then describe and prescribe a number of steps you can take with regard to limiting the risks of investing in a crazy world.

Risky Business

We live in a radically indeterminate world. Not only do we not know what will happen next, in principle—according to modern physics—*we cannot know what will happen next.* This is true whether we are walking down the street or investing our hard-earned money for retirement. For a great description of how and why you can't know what will happen next with regard to particular equity investments, see Burton Malkiel's fabulous *A Random Walk Down Wall Street* (first published in 1993 and as of this writing in its tenth edition).

Earlier, in Chapter 4, the notions of *endogenous* and *exogenous* risk were reviewed. Endogenous risk refers to risk that originates from within, while exogenous risk comes from outside your base model. Suppose, for example, you work at a mountain resort and are on the ski patrol, and it is your job to warn others where there might be an avalanche. Well, while you don't know if and when an avalanche will happen, you do know that there is a risk one will happen, and you can assess the likely factors of this endogenous risk.

However, an exogenous risk could also be present. Suppose a meteorite lands in a section of the mountain that you had thought was impervious to an avalanche, and it causes an avalanche. That meteorite is an exogenous risk, one outside of what anyone would have reasonably expected, yet in fact such a thing would be possible in this scenario. Unfortunately, it is very difficult—or perhaps, again, in principle impossible—to be aware of exogenous risks before they happen. That is, we don't know what we don't know, and at a certain level, we can't know what we don't know.

So, while investing is ultimately always a risky business—without risk, there would be no reward—it is incumbent upon us to do what we can do to limit our risk. This means being aware of the nature of risk, working with someone who is also aware of the nature of risk, and taking a number of proactive steps such as the ones that will be described in the last section of this appendix.

Are You Prepared for the Future? (Expanded from Chapter 5)

The ideas presented in this book are risky in any economic environment. My greatest concern as an author is that investors may draw conclusions about their ability to capture the spread based on data from their most recent past—perhaps by using average risk, return, and correlation assumptions they have recently experienced as the basis for their future return assumptions. Too often this is what the financial industry and academia do in their models. My concern is that this could be a terrible mistake as this past may not represent our future. My goal is to fundamentally change the way you look at the world with respect to risk.

It is imperative to assess recent U.S. economic history in order to gain an understanding that can help provide clarity. I can tell you for certain that most of the data from the recent past cannot repeat itself—and in many cases, could be the opposite over the next 30 years. To prepare for the future, therefore, alternate economic histories must be considered.[1]

From 1980 to 2013 interest rates have generally moved from high to low, inflation has moved from high to low, and government debt has moved from low to high. While I am not saying that interest rates cannot move lower, the economic phenomena of rates moving from the midteens to the 2 percent (and lower) range cannot repeat itself at a similar magnitude.

In the past 30 years, both consumer debt and government spending have moved from low to high. Government debt went from a relatively low nominal amount in 1980 to a massive figure today (on an absolute and relative basis) approaching $17 trillion.[2] In the early 1980s, the Baby Boomer generation was just hitting its workplace stride and was fully employed; today, the same generation is well on its way to being fully retired. These data trends also cannot be repeated in the next 30 years to the same degree.

Knowing that we are at a different starting place, I feel then that investors need to examine multiple other economic histories to learn from them to try to get a sense of what our future could look like. I am certainly not alone in the view that economic history is important to study and understand. From *This Time is Different* by Rogoff and Reinhart to Congressional Budget Office, the Office of Management and Budget, the United States Treasury, and most notably, the International Monetary Fund in its 2012 World Economic Outlook entitled *Coping with High Debt and Sluggish Growth*, this concept of a different starting place is being explored in detail.[3]

So, if we are looking at alternate economic histories, where might we look? Economic history in Japan, Argentina, and Europe might illustrate some challenges the United States could face in the next periods of time.

- The deflation Japan experienced from 1980–2000, which would be roughly equivalent to the Dow Jones trading at about 7,000 and interest rates staying under 2 percent. This resulted in the gradual collapse of the Japanese economy, often referred to as the Lost Decade.[4]
- The inflation, hyperinflation, and devaluation Argentina experienced in the 1990–2000 period.[5]
- The European economic crisis, characterized by weak equities, higher interest rates, and contracting GDP (Spain, Greece, and Italy).

This is not a comprehensive list either. Investors should study France after World War I, England after World War II (and in particular to the cause and impact of them losing their status as a reserve currency), and the crisis in East Asia in the late 1990s.[6] A review of history suggests that once countries hit a significant debt issue, the problem is usually ultimately resolved through a combination of default, growth, inflation, and devaluation.[7]

There are key differences between the economic situation of the United States and each of the other countries just mentioned. However, there are many similarities and there are important lessons to be learned from economic history. Although it is unlikely that the fate of the United States will be exactly like any of these case studies, it is also highly unlikely, if not impossible, for the next 30 years to look like the past 30 years. Our perspective must shift.

So, what might the next time period look like? And how should you be positioning assets to ensure that you are ready? If I have yet to grab your attention, the lessons from the fiscal cliff and the sensitivity of our economy to shocks should surely shift your thinking. Let's consider the following: Why was the fiscal cliff debate in 2012 a big deal? And what does it really mean?

The fiscal cliff debate represented a potential sharp decline in the budget deficit that would have occurred due to the increased taxes and reduced spending required by previously enacted laws. Many economists felt the fiscal cliff would have triggered changes in GDP, which is a common measure of how our economy is growing. GDP is calculated with this simple equation: GDP = consumption (C) + investment (I) + government (G) + (exports − imports). We need to remember that our economy is very sensitive to even small changes in GDP.

The fiscal cliff was a big deal in 2012 because most economists felt that the mandatory sequestration would have led to a decrease in government spending (G), and the increase in taxes would have led to a decrease in consumption (C). Although estimates varied, the concern was that the fiscal cliff could have potentially caused a significant recession during an already weak recovery. Some were concerned that if GDP was naturally growing at say 2 percent and the contraction shaved 4 percent off of the economy, then all else equal 2% − 4% = −2%. Most importantly, people were concerned that it could be enough to shift our economy from growth to contraction. The debate largely centered around whether we need to be taking steps to address our long-term issues now, or if we should be "pushing through" this period and implement the changes later.[8]

What has happened to the United States's debt and deficits over the past decade is not insignificant. What is worse is that the country didn't see it coming. In fact, the Congressional Budget Office (CBO) predicted the opposite, projecting a cumulative surplus of $5.6 trillion between 2002 and 2011. In actuality, the United States ran a $6.1 trillion cumulative deficit—or debt increase—of $11.7 trillion. This was a stunning miss![9]

In 2000, the United States had approximately $5.7 trillion of debt and was running a budget surplus of about $236 billion. In 2013, the United States has more than $16.5 trillion of debt and deficits of $400 billion + per year predicted for as far as we can see into the future.[10] After such a dramatic increase in debt and deficits, one might intuitively think that interest rates would have moved higher, because those buying bonds are lending to an inherently riskier entity. It turns out, however, that interest rates have actually moved lower.[11]

This understanding of the economic reality in the United States should help us frame several key questions, including

- Why were investors demanding an average rate of return of roughly 6 percent in 2000 but are now willing to accept rates under 2 percent?
- Were rates too high in 2000 and were investors being massively overcompensated for their risk? Or, are rates too low today and investors are being massively undercompensated for their risk? Is somebody wrong?

So, let's employ a stress test to evaluate the sensitivity of the U.S. economy to shocks. A good place to start is by reviewing key assumptions made by the CBO, including that our economy will have stable to moderately increasing interest rates (never crossing 5 percent), decreasing unemployment, consistent GDP growth (growing by approximately 62 percent over the next 10 years) and that the Federal Reserve will keep inflation low and stable. They also assume that federal revenues will increase by approximately 100 percent over the next decade.[12]

These assumptions led the CBO to declare that the United States will have approximately $20 trillion of debt in 2023 and will be running annual deficits of approximately $1 trillion.[13] Notice that this is just debt held by the public; it does not include any of the unfunded obligations that the government has to its workers and citizens nor does it include multiple "off-balance-sheet" obligations.[14]

But what if the CBO is wrong? Each of their assumptions should be stress-tested. For example, what if Nominal GDP averages closer to 2 or 3 percent, what are the implications on revenues and on our debt to GDP ratios? Or what if interest rates go up at a faster rate? This shock is an easier example to show so it is a good place to start.

If one assumes that the government's average cost of borrowing moves from 2 percent to 6 percent on the $11.5 trillion of debt held by the public, then the resulting increase in interest expense would be conceptually 4 percent multiplied by $11.5 trillion, resulting in an additional $460 billion per year in expense. With all else equal, this would lead to three economic possibilities: Revenue must go up (tax increases); government spending would decrease; or the deficit would increase.

The problem is that $460 billion is a really big number. In fact, according to David Wessel, "wages and benefits for everyone from the President to air force pilots to postal service clerks cost $435 billion in 2011."[15] This means that if you fired every federal employee, including all military service personnel, you would still be running the same deficit and have the same debt. Actually, you would in fact be sinking by about $25 billion per year.

Clearly it can't all come from cuts in wages. The questions then become where the cuts would be coming from, what are the offsetting revenues, and then what would happen to GDP as a result. We can look to lessons from the fiscal cliff to try to understand this scenario. Recall how difficult it was to address a $100 billion per year issue. This shock is over four times that.

All else equal, increasing taxes leads to a decrease in GDP, and a decrease in government spending results in a decrease in GDP. This implies a highly leveraged country could face a scenario of rising interest rates and contracting GDP. Rolling it onto the deficit may end up having other adverse consequences. All of this could also have implications on inflation as well as on the value of our currency.

Other people may balk at this, believing that interest rates can't go up because the Federal Reserve doesn't want them to. Oddly, with interest rates near generational lows, one might think that the United States is borrowing money long term and locking in low rates. It turns out, however, that of the marketable securities held by the public as of September 30, 2012, $6.255 trillion (or 58 percent) will mature within the next four years. In addition to financing this $6.255 trillion, we will also have to sell enough debt to finance our ongoing deficit.[16]

So in a period of potentially rising interest rates and potentially rising national debt, our base case is to sell approximately $10 trillion of our bonds to somebody. How exactly will this take place and who is going to buy all this debt?

Roughly $5.6 trillion of U.S. debt is held by foreigners. Other nations hold more of our debt today than the total level of outstanding debt in 2000. An event that is quite significant occurred in 2012: China reduced its outstanding holdings of Treasury securities.[17] If we know that the United States must continue to finance debt and that some of the biggest buyers are becoming sellers, we must ask ourselves if it is not at least possible that interest rates could rise.

Tying this back to the previous discussions on countries, it is interesting to look at Spain recently. Spain's economic environment over the last few years could represent some of the threats in our future. Spain has been facing increasing taxes causing consumption (C) to decline, austerity measures have triggered a decrease in government spending (G), and investments (I) are falling due to a lack of confidence. This has, of course, led to a contraction in their GDP. At the same time, global markets have expressed concern and interest rates are generally higher. Unemployment has trended up, housing prices have trended down.[18]

None of this is intended to be a specific forecast, but rather to discuss different economic environments we could face. The point is the possibility of a scenario in which you are faced broadly with rising interest rates, contracting GDP, falling equity prices, rising unemployment, and falling housing prices has tremendous implications not only on your investment strategy, but also on your strategic debt philosophy. The same is true for a period of extended deflation, or a period of inflation or hyperinflation. In all cases use caution when using recent data and make sure your scenarios consider the wide range of outcomes that we could face.

> The past 30 years of economic history in the United States cannot repeat itself. Investors must not use this time period as the basis for investment decisions.

In light of these points, investors should position their portfolios for the different potential environments we could face by addressing five main points:

1. Embrace a goal-based approach to asset allocation and get your account structure right.
2. Play both offense and defense.
3. Reframe your view of the world and eliminate home bias.
4. Proactively stress-test your portfolios and examine your debt ratio and debt strategies.
5. Include antifragile characteristics in your portfolio.

Investors may want to consider embracing a goal-based approach to asset allocation and to get your account structure right. Investors typically have three objectives: *Safety* is measured as keeping pace with inflation; *core* is measured as inflation + 4 percent returns, and *tactical* is for those assets that investors have for which they are willing to take on more risk for the potential of more return.

At a minimum, investors should consider having a three- to six-month cash reserve for emergencies. Any additional cash needs for the next year also be in cash. Any financial needs over the next five years may be invested with a goal of safety. From here, I recommend that you work with your financial advisor to examine your needs and risk tolerance in order to determine the right weighting between safety, core, and tactical.

Your financial advisor should have a risk dashboard that enables him or her to make proactive investment changes by utilizing the latest technology to accomplish precision investing, account level defined objectives, and dynamic rebalancing.[19] None of this is possible without the right account structure. Assets should be held in an integrated account where the manager is able to do all of the aforementioned.

Portfolios should be dynamically rebalanced based on their stated goals and the relative movement between asset classes.

I'm not advocating that investors go to cash, and likewise, investors should not rush to put all their money in bonds. There are instances in history of investors who have held $20 million in bonds only to find these bonds to be worth only $6 million—within a very short period of time.[20] Advisors need to spend an extensive amount of time testing each of the tenets of how we model our portfolios and what shapes our perspective. Just as important as it is to test for the downside, investors must be positioned to participate in the possibility of continued upside in higher-risk assets. Investors must play both offense and defense to win!

Investors must also be cognizant of home bias, the process of overweighting one's home country in asset allocation. It is a major flaw in most portfolios. Although it is an extreme example, Greece illustrates the pain of home bias. It didn't matter if a person held 60 percent Greek stocks, 40 percent Greek bonds or 40 percent Greek stocks, 60 percent Greek bonds. Size, style, and company selection were of little relevance. What mattered was how much the investor had in Greece (or, actually, how much the investor had outside of Greece). Not surprisingly, I typically see that U.S. investors have approximately

---

TRULY DIVERSIFIED?

Many portfolios that I encounter are somewhere in the range of 70 percent equities/30 percent bonds to 30 percent equities/70 percent bonds. Their bonds tend to be between 95 percent and 100 percent in the United States, and their stocks tend to be between 70 percent and 90 percent in the United States. When you do the math on this, most U.S. investors have over 80 percent of their assets in the United States (and generally over 90 percent!). If you have an allocation such as this, then I would suggest that you consider studying economic history more aggressively. It is full of examples where those who exhibited home bias were severely punished when their county entered an economic crisis.

85 percent or more of their money in the United States, denominated in U.S. dollars.

Investors must continually evaluate the world and the asset classes they choose to hold. Corporate, high-yield, and municipal bond positions need to be carefully analyzed versus the multiple alternative economic environments that we could face. Similarly, long-term Treasury bonds, intermediate Treasuries, and Treasury Inflation Protected Securities (TIPS) need to be tested for a range of outcomes. Investors who continue to hold these asset classes need to consider both their fundamentals and their supply and demand characteristics over the next five years.

Crucially, your debt and corresponding debt ratio needs to be carefully examined and stress-tested against multiple scenarios. Your financial advisor should have access to software that enables him or her to model the impact of another 2008, a terrorist strike, a Greek-type event, and so on.

Finally, it is imperative that an investor's strategy includes antifragile characteristics. Nassim Taleb coined the phrase *antifragile*.[21] Antifragile is

---

RISK OR OPPORTUNITY?

The economic situation that our country is in creates a unique set of risks and a unique set of opportunities. A lot of time has been spent discussing the risks the United States faces. Traditionally debt problems are resolved through default, growth, inflation, or devaluation—or a combination of each.

The opportunity is that we can proactively position around these risks. For example, there are countries in the world that have almost none of our entitlement obligations, they have a lower debt ratio, are running small deficits (and even surpluses), and pay a higher rate of interest. Mathematically if I invest in a foreign bond paying 3 percent and the dollar falls by 3 percent, then all else equal I am up 6 percent. If I borrowed in dollars at 2 percent, then I captured a spread of 4 percent. The risks and opportunities this presents should be discussed in detail with your advisors.

something that thrives and grows when exposed to volatility, randomness, and disorder, and actually becomes stronger as stress is applied. This concept can be expressed in investing. In these times, there are some assets that should be held for their antifragile characteristics. These include, but are not limited to, deep out-of-the-money options that can act as a form of insurance from some of the extreme events we could face. These may or may not be appropriate for you and the risks and potential benefits should be discussed in detail with your advisors.

This is a very complicated world. I encourage you to challenge your portfolios by stress-testing them. Similarly, it is beneficial to challenge your advisors—stress-test them, too! It is imperative to ask tough questions, expect detailed answers, and most importantly, not be surprised by (or unprepared for) what the future brings.

Summary Steps Worth Considering

Given the level of risk and uncertainty we are always facing, the following steps and precautions are well worth considering, especially if you chose to adopt any of the Strategic Debt Practices or ideas from this book:

- Make sure you are working with a *competent financial advisor* with a solid understanding of economic history.
- Working with that advisor, adopt a *long-term goals-based approach to asset allocation*.
- Keep in mind when making asset allocation decisions that you have to *play both offense and defense*, as your investment and financial choices could be wrong, early, or late.
- Make sure you have the *right kind of account structure*, one that is nimble and tax aware.
- Consider adopting a *world-neutral view*, that is, do not overfavor investments in your home country. United States investors should be mindful that the United States only makes up only a small percentage (15–20 percent) of the world's total economy; there are many opportunities elsewhere, and simple prudence and principles of diversification (don't have all your eggs in one basket) dictate that you should not be overconcentrated in any one country.

- *Stress-test your portfolio* for a broad range of outcomes; keep testing so that virtually no event is unexpected or exogenous.
- *Never, ever, underestimate the importance of liquidity*—of having cash on hand or being able to access it immediately.
- If you can afford it, consider taking out a kind of *insurance against disastrous economic downturns* by positioning a small percentage of your total holdings against the markets in various ways.
- Never forget that *taking on any leverage*, especially for wealth amplification purposes, *increases your overall risk* of encountering substantial financial distress.
- Never forget that *drawing on an ABLF also increases your risk*, and that you must carefully monitor your coverage ratios.

Is this a risky world? Yes. Is investing a risky business? Yes. But failing to invest for the future is itself a kind of investment in the likelihood of your financial situation substantially deteriorating. Ultimately, most of us will want to, and will have to, take action. Just make sure that action is done with as much awareness of the risks involved as possible, and with as informed a long-term perspective as possible. Good luck.

Official Statement of Disclosure and Understanding

(You knew it had to be somewhere in this book.)

This book does not provide individually tailored investment advice. It has been prepared without regard to the circumstances and objectives of those who receive it. This book contains general information only, does not take account of the specific circumstances of any reader, and should not be relied upon as authoritative or taken in substitution for the exercise of judgment by any recipient.

Each reader should consider the appropriateness of any investment decision as it regards to his or her own circumstances, the full range of information available, and appropriate professional advice.

The author recommends that readers independently evaluate particular investments and strategies, and encourages them to seek a financial advisor's advice. Under no circumstances should this publication be construed as a solicitation to buy or sell any security or to participate in any trading or investment strategy, nor should this book, or any part of it, form the basis of, or be relied on in connection with, any contract or commitment whatsoever.

The value of and income from investments may vary because of changes in interest rates or foreign exchange rates, securities prices or market indexes, operational or financial conditions of companies, and geopolitical or other factors.

Past performance is not necessarily a guide to future performance. Estimates of future performance are based on assumptions that may not be realized. The information and opinions in the book constitute judgment as of the date of publication, have been compiled and arrived at from sources believed to be reliable and in good faith (but no representation or warranty, express or implied, is made as to their accuracy, completeness, or correctness), and are subject to change without notice.

Investing with leverage contains multiple risks, including, but not limited to, interest rate risk, greater volatility risk, liquidity risk, call provision risk, rollover risk, and the risk of a total loss of capital.

The information provided is based on tax laws currently in effect and is subject to change. There is a possibility that current tax legislation will be amended or repealed in the future. In that case, the outcome of these planning ideas may not be as advantageous. None of the information herein is to be considered tax advice. All ideas are intended to represent tax facts at the time of publication and are subject to change without notice. All ideas must be reviewed by your tax legal and financial advisors based on your individual situation.

Tax information contained in this presentation is general and not exhaustive by nature. It is not intended or written to be used, and cannot be used, by any taxpayer for the purpose of avoiding U.S. federal tax laws. Pursuant to the rules of professional conduct set forth in Circular 230, as promulgated by the United States Department of the Treasury, nothing contained in this book was intended or written to be used by any taxpayer for the purpose of avoiding penalties that may be imposed on the taxpayer by the Internal Revenue Service, and it cannot be used by any taxpayer for such purpose. Federal and state tax laws are complex and constantly changing. Investors should always consult their tax advisor for information concerning their individual situation.

No one, without the express prior written permission of the author, may refer to any of the debt, investment, or tax strategies found in this book.

The author does not accept any liability whatsoever for any loss or damage arising from any use of this book and its contents. All data and information and opinions expressed herein are subject to change without notice.

With Respect to ABLFs

ABLFs are a securities-based loan, which can be risky and are not suitable for all investors. Before opening an account, you should understand the following risks:

- The firm can call the loan at any time and for any reason.
- Sufficient collateral must be maintained to support your loan(s) and to take future advances.
- You may have to deposit additional cash and/or eligible securities on short notice.
- Some or all of your securities may be sold without prior notice in order to maintain account equity at required maintenance levels. You will not be entitled to choose the securities that will be sold. These actions may interrupt your long-term investment strategy and may result in adverse tax consequences or in additional fees being assessed.
- Firms typically reserve the right not to fund any advance request due to insufficient collateral or for any other reason.
- Firms can increase your collateral maintenance requirements at any time without notice.
- There may be minimum line sizes and minimum initial draws.
- Disbursements are subject to your available credit and are at the sole discretion of the firm.
- Annual fees typically apply for Standby Letters of Credit, if issued. Standby Letters of Credit carry issuance fees based on the issued amount of the Letter of Credit and are due in advance.

- For brokerage firms, ABLFs are typically offered by the bank affiliated with the issuing brokerage firm.
- Credit lines are often subject to credit approval.
- You should consult your legal and tax advisors regarding the legal and tax implications of borrowing using securities as collateral for a loan.
- For a full discussion of the risks associated with borrowing using securities as collateral, you should review the Loan Disclosure Statement that will be included in your application package.

ABLFs can be either what are called purpose or nonpurpose loans. A *nonpurpose loan* is a line of credit or loan that is based on the eligible securities held in a brokerage account. It can be used for any suitable purpose except to purchase, trade, or carry securities or repay debt that was used to purchase, trade, or carry securities, and should not be deposited into a brokerage account. A *purpose loan*, or margin loan offered by a brokerage firm, is a revolving line of credit based on securities held in a brokerage account. These loans are primarily used to purchase securities but can be used for any other purpose. The text is not intended to imply that having an ABLF is guaranteed liquidity. It is important to note that many ABLFs are not committed facilities. Therefore, a lender has no obligation to make an advance and can reject any advance request from a borrower in its sole discretion.

ABLFs could in fact actually increase your risk of distress. If you have an ABLF and the market drops (including the securities securing your loan), you could be forced into a margin call with no additional securities/collateral to deposit and in a situation where you don't have liquid funds to pay down the loan. Accordingly, you could be forced to sell the securities collateral at that time, which if the market is depressed, would be at a bad price and potentially trigger tax consequences.

ABLFs generally are structured as demand facilities, which means that the institution offering the loan can demand repayment at any time. Also, the lender usually maintains the right to liquidate the securities held collateral at any time. You must work with your advisors to understand and mitigate these risks.

All examples within the book assume that credit is available, securities are eligible, and the lender is willing to continue advancing money.

Additional Important Notes

Securities-Based Loans: Borrowing against securities may not be suitable for everyone. You should be aware that securities-based loans (ABLFs) involve a high degree of risk and that market conditions can magnify any potential for loss. Most importantly, you need to understand an ABLF is not a committed facility, the lender has no obligation to make an advance, and therefore an ABLF *does not offer a guaranteed liquidity solution.*

Although your lender may not have a cost in establishing an ABLF, you must visit with your tax, legal, and financial advisors before implementing any of these ideas. Accordingly, there may be professional advisory fees in pursuing the ideas expressed in this material.

Taxes: Tax laws are complex and subject to change. This material was not intended or written to be used for the purpose of avoiding tax penalties that may be imposed on the taxpayer. Individuals are encouraged to consult their tax and legal advisors (a) before establishing a retirement plan or account, and (b) regarding any potential tax, ERISA, and related consequences of any investments made under such plan or account.

Point of view: The views expressed herein are those of the author. All opinions are subject to change without notice. Neither the information provided nor any opinion expressed constitutes a solicitation for the purchase or sale of any security. Past performance is no guarantee of future results.

Strategies: This material does not provide individually tailored investment advice. It has been prepared without regard to the individual financial circumstances and objectives of persons who receive it. The strategies and/or investments discussed in this material may not be suitable for all investors. The author recommends that investors independently evaluate particular investments and strategies, and encourages investors to seek the advice of a financial advisor and their tax and legal advisors. The appropriateness of a particular investment or strategy will depend on an investor's individual circumstances and objectives.

Asset allocation: Asset allocation and diversification do not guarantee a profit or protect against a loss.

Bonds: Bonds are subject to interest rate risk. When interest rates rise, bond prices fall; generally the longer a bond's maturity, the more sensitive it is to this risk. Bonds may also be subject to call risk, which is the risk that the issuer will redeem the debt at its option, fully or partially, before the scheduled maturity date. The market value of debt instruments may fluctuate, and proceeds from sales prior to maturity may be more or less than the amount originally invested or the maturity value due to changes in market conditions or changes in the credit quality of the issuer. Bonds are subject to the credit risk of the issuer. This is the risk that the issuer might be unable to make interest and/or principal payments on a timely basis. Bonds are also subject to reinvestment risk, which is the risk that principal and/or interest payments from a given investment may be reinvested at a lower interest rate. International bonds are subject to these and other additional risks such as increased risk of default, greater volatility, and currency risk.

Municipal bonds: Interest in muni bonds is generally exempt from federal income tax. However, some bonds may be subject to the AMT. Typically, state tax exemption applies if securities are issued within one's state of residence and, local tax exemption typically applies if securities are issued within one's city of residence. Bonds are affected by a number of risks, including fluctuations in interest rates, credit risk, and prepayment risk. In general, as prevailing interest rates rise, fixed income securities prices will fall. Bonds face credit risk if a decline in an issuer's credit rating, or creditworthiness, causes a bond's price to decline. Finally, bonds can be subject to prepayment risk. When interest rates fall, an issuer may choose to borrow money at a lower interest rate, while paying off its previously issued bonds. As a consequence, underlying bonds will lose the interest payments from the investment and will be forced to reinvest in a market where prevailing interest rates are lower than when the initial investment was made. *Note:* High-yield bonds are subject to additional risks such as increased risk of default and greater volatility because of the lower credit quality of the issues.

Equities: Equity securities may fluctuate in response to news on companies, industries, market conditions, and general economic environment. Companies paying dividends can reduce or cut payouts at any time.

Case studies: The case studies presented are for educational and illustrative purposes only and do not indicate future performance. Past performance is no guarantee of future results. Investment results may vary. The investment strategies and products and services presented are not appropriate for every investor. Individual clients should review with their financial advisors the terms and conditions and risks involved with specific products or services. Neither the information provided nor any opinion expressed constitutes a solicitation for the purchase or sale of any security. All of the illustrations throughout the book are hypothetical and not intended to demonstrate the performance of any specific security, product, or investment strategy.

Home loan—mortgage: Proceeds from mortgage loan transactions including initial draws and advances from HELOCs are not permitted to be used to purchase trade or carry marginable securities, repay margin debt, or to make payments on any amounts owed under a note or HELOC loan agreement.

LIBOR and interest-only loans: An interest-only LIBOR loan is not for everyone. Your interest rate can increase and monthly payments can increase every one or six months, depending on the index you choose. Additionally, your monthly payments will generally increase when the interest-only period ends because you will be repaying principal and interest over the remaining loan term.

CDs: CDs are insured by the FDIC, an independent agency of the U.S. government, up to a maximum amount of $250,000 (including principal and interest) for all deposits held in the same insurable capacity (e.g., individual account, joint account) per CD depository. For more information visit the FDIC website at www.fdic.gov and talk to your own advisors about what products may or may not be available to you. [22]

INVESTMENTS AND INSURANCE PRODUCTS: NOT FDIC INSURED • NOT A BANK DEPOSIT • NOT INSURED BY ANY FEDERAL GOVERNMENT AGENCY • NOT BANK GUARANTEED • MAY LOSE VALUE

Notes

1. The notion that there are three distinct periods in time, the past 30 years, today, and the next 30 years, is inspired from a presentation given by Jeffrey Rosenberg, Chief Investment Strategist for Fixed Income, Blackrock, at the Barron's Top 100 Conference, fall 2012. Lectures from David Wessel, Luigi Zingales, Ed Lazear, and Martin Feldstein, Paul Krugman, Gary Becker, and Naill Ferguson in the fall of 2012 and into Summer of 2013 as well as a lecture at Harvard University in the Summer of 2011 inspired some of the views expressed in this section. Readers looking for additional detail should familiarize themselves with their work.

2. "U.S. National Debt Clock." *U.S. Debt Clock.* N.p., 2013. www.usdebtclock .org.

3. Carmen M. Reinhart and Kenneth S. Rogoff, *This Time Is Different: Eight Centuries of Financial Folly* (Princeton, NJ: Princeton University Press, 2009).

   Congressional Budget Office. *Budget and Economic Outlook: Fiscal Years 2013 to 2023.* Washington D.C.:, 2013. http://cbo.gov/sites/default/files/cbofiles /attachments/43907-BudgetOutlook.pdf.

   Office of Management and Budget. *Fiscal Year 2014 Budget of the U.S. Government.* Washington D.C.:, 2013. www.whitehouse.gov/omb/budget.

   Government Accountability Office. *Financial Audit: Bureau of the Public Debt's Fiscal Years 2012 and 2011 Schedules of Federal Debt.* Washington D.C.:, 2012. www.treasurydirect.gov/govt/reports/pd/feddebt/feddebt_ann2012.pdf.

   "World Economic Outlook October 2012: Coping with High Debt and Sluggish Growth." *World Economic and Financial Surveys.* International Monetary Fund, n.d. www.imf.org/external/pubs/ft/weo/2012/02/pdf/text.pdf.

4. In actuality the Nikkei 225 reached an all-time high of 38,916 in December of 1989 and then traded below 10,000 as recently as 2012. For the purposes of this reference I am more focused on the time period of the early 2000s when it was in the 20,000 range (and was flat for the past 10 years—similar to what the S&P is doing today) to falling by 50 percent eight years later— and longer. The CFA Institute has a great discussion on the Japanese Debt Crisis and there are several public websites that let you track the historic performance of the index.

   http://blogs.cfainstitute.org/investor/2012/04/19/the-japanese-debt-crisis-has-japan-passed-the-point-of-no-return/; http://blogs.cfainstitute. org/investor/2012/04/20/the-japanese-debt-crisis-part-2-when-does-japan-cross-the-event-horizon/.

5. Ramon Moreno, "Learning from Argentina's Crisis," *Economic Research*, Federal Reserve Bank of San Fransisco, October 18, 2002.

   www.frbsf.org/economic-research/publications/economic-letter/2002/october/learning-from-argentina-crisis/.

6. Ramon Moreno "What Caused East Asia's Financial Crisis?" *Economic Research*, Federal Reserve Bank of San Fransisco, August 7, 1998.

   www.frbsf.org/economic-research/publications/economic-letter/1998/august/what-caused-east-asia-financial-crisis/.

7. This refers to ideas expressed in the book *This Time is Different* as well as information in the following presentation:

   Reinhart and Rogoff, *This Time is Different*.

   S. Ali Abbas, Nazim Belhocine, et al., "Historical Patterns and Dynamics of Public Debt: Evidence from a New Database," *Fiscal Affairs Department: International Monetary Fund*. International Monetary Fund, June 7, 2011.

   www.imf.org/external/np/seminars/eng/2010/eui/pdf/elg.pdf

8. It is also outside of the scope of this appendix to fully cover the impact of changes in GDP but for perspective, in advanced economies in particular, a 2 percent contraction in GDP is typically considered a significant contraction and growth over 2 percent is considered to be meaningful growth. As we look back across countries and throughout time, movements of more than 5 percent up or down often represent some of the most meaningful and/or largest inflection points in a country's economic history. To capture the scope of this debate type in "fiscal cliff debate" and review some of the 20 million+ hits.

9. Congressional Budget Office. *Changes in CBO's Baseline Projections Since January 2001*. Washington D.C.:, 2012. www.cbo.gov/sites/default/files/cbofiles/attachments/06-07-ChangesSince2001Baseline.pdf.

10. Office of Management and Budget. *Budget for Fiscal Year 2013: Historical Tables*. Washington D.C.:, 2012. www.whitehouse.gov/sites/default/files/omb/budget/fy2013/assets/hist.pdf.

    Congressional Budget Office. *Budget and Economic Outlook: Fiscal Years 2013 to 2023*. Washington D.C.:, 2013. http://cbo.gov/sites/default/files/cbofiles/attachments/43907-BudgetOutlook.pdf

11. Government Accountability Office. *Financial Audit: Bureau of the Public Debt's Fiscal Years 2012 and 2011 Schedules of Federal Debt*. Washington D.C.:, 2012. See Page 21. www.treasurydirect.gov/govt/reports/pd/feddebt/feddebt_ann2012.pdf.

12. Congressional Budget Office. *Budget and Economic Outlook: Fiscal Years 2013 to 2023*. Washington D.C.:, 2013.

13. Ibid.

14. Chris Cox and Bill Archer, "Why $16 Trillion Only Hints at the True U.S. Debt," *Wall Street Journal*, November 28, 2012. http://online.wsj.com/article/SB10001424127887323353204578127374039087636.html.

15. David Wessel, *Red Ink: Inside the High-Stakes Politics of the Federal Budget* (New York: Crown Publishing Group, 2012), 22.

16. A complete schedule of the U.S. Debt maturities can be found here: United States Department of the Treasury, *Monthly Statement of the Public Debt of The United States*. Washington D.C.:, 2012. www.treasurydirect.gov/govt/reports/pd/mspd/2012/opdm122012.pdf.

17. Details on the previous three sentences can be found here.

    United States Department of The Treasury. *Major Foreign Holders of Treasury Securities*. Washington D.C.:, 2013. www.treasury.gov/resource-center/data-chart-center/tic/Documents/mfh.txt.

    United States Department of the Treasury. *Resource Center*. Washington D.C.:, 2013. www.treasury.gov/resource-center/Pages/default.aspx.

18. Note that Spain's GDP in 2010 was less than that of 2007, and its 2013 GDP is likely to be under 2007 as well. Note that the 2012 GDP in Spain, Italy, Greece, and Portugal is under 2008 levels, and that Japan's GDP in 2009 is under the 1995 level. Japan's 2010 GDP is nominally over that of 1995. The point is that the CBO's assumption of constant GDP growth is perhaps a difficult assumption based on what we have seen in other markets. "Data: GDP (Current US Dollars)." *The World Bank*. The World Bank, 2013. http://data.worldbank.org/indicator/NY.GDP.MKTP.CD?page=3.

19. The ideas expressed in this sentence are directly inspired by a lecture that Leo Tilman gave at the Barron's Top 100 Conference in the fall of 2012. Mr. Tilman is the president of L.M. Tilman & Co., serves on the faculty of Columbia University, and is the author of *Financial Darwinism* (Hoboken, NJ: John Wiley & Sons, 2008).

20. The Bank of Greece, "Government Benchmark Bond Prices and Yields," Bank of Greece, May 2013.

    www.bankofgreece.gr/Pages/en/Statistics/rates_markets/titloieldimosiou/titloieldimosiou.aspx.

21. Nassim Nicholas Taleb, *Antifragile: Things That Gain from Disorder* (New York: Random House, 2012).

22. The information in this appendix is to be considered in a holistic way as a part of the book and not to be considered on a stand-alone basis. This

includes, but is not limited to, the discussion of risks of each of these ideas as well as all of the disclaimers throughout the book. The material is presented with a goal of encouraging thoughtful conversation and rigorous debate on the risks and potential benefits of the concepts between you and your advisors based on your unique situation, risk tolerance, and goals.

Appendix D

Some Examples of Ideal Debt Ratios*

T his appendix will help to frame the concept of *optimal* by
sketching out what a number of different optimal debt ratios
look like in practice. Since some of these materials are a bit more

---

advanced, we will use the same format we used at the end of Chapter 5, which is to lay out two balance sheets in a side-by-side comparison. We will start out with a review of a case study from Chapter 5 and then continue on to increasingly more advanced scenarios and concepts.

Scenario 1: "I'm an Accumulator— No Debt for Me!"

(This is the same scenario for Jane earlier reviewed in Chapter 5.)

In the optimal scenario, on the right of Table D.1, Jane

- Generates $16,000 more per year in income, which is equivalent to increasing her rate of return by 53.3 percent.
- Gets a significant tax deduction (the benefit of this is accounted for in her after-tax cost of debt).

Table D.1 Scenario 1: "I'm an Accumulator—No Debt for Me!"

Existing—Jane Scenario A			Optimal—Jane Scenario B		
Assets		**Liabilities**	**Assets**		**Liabilities**
Real estate			Real estate		
Home	$ 500,000	—	Home	$ 500,000	400,000
Investments			Investments		
Portfolio	500,000	—	Portfolio	900,000	—
Total	1,000,000	—	Total	1,400,000	400,000
Net worth	$1,000,000	**0% debt ratio**	Net worth	$1,000,000	**29% debt ratio**
		Income Perspective			
Portfolio income	6%	$30,000	Portfolio income	6%	$54,000
After-tax cost of debt	2%	—	After-tax cost of debt	2%	(8,000)
Net income		$30,000	Net income		$46,000
			Additional income compared to existing		**$16,000**

- Is eligible for an ABLF that is 80 percent higher and likely priced at a lower rate.
- Is not subject to a forced margin call because her debt is structured against her home.
- Can pay off her debt anytime she doesn't like this strategy.

If Jane reinvests the additional $16,000 at the same 6 percent for five years, she will generate a total of approximately $90,000 in additional value versus the no-debt scenario on the left.

Looking forward:

- Notice that Jane's future income should go to her portfolio, not to her house (and her debt ratio will likely continue to fall as a result!).
- In the event that Jane needs to buy a car, pay a significant tax bill, or do a major home improvement or finance a hobby, then she may look toward using her ABLF.

Scenario 2: More Established, Still Working

Here we have a scenario that represents many people who are more established yet still working. You can imagine that the husband and wife have a $500,000 home somewhere up north, and they have a $1.5 million home somewhere that is warm. They have an investment portfolio worth $4 million. Their net worth is about $6 million.

One clear possibility is that they could have no debt at all. An alternative optimal scenario is that upon purchase of that second home, they could step in and do a $1.5 million mortgage (100 percent financing, see Chapter 6) versus that property. Table D.2 compares the two.

Optimal scenario analysis: In the optimal scenario they have $5.5 million in a core portfolio and $7.5 million of total assets along with $1.5 million of debt.

- Their net worth is $7.5 million − $1.5 million = $6 million.
  - An individual or family's net worth never changes because of financing.
- Their debt ratio is a conservative 20 percent.
  - This is derived from dividing $1.5 million by $7.5 million.

Table D.2 Scenario 2: More Established, Still Working

Near Retirement—Scenario A			Near Retirement—Scenario B		
Assets		**Liabilities**	**Assets**		**Liabilities**
Real estate			Real estate		
Home	$ 500,000	—	Home 2	$ 500,000	
Home 2	1,500,000			1,500,000	$1,500,000
Investments			Investments		
Portfolio	4,000,000	—	Portfolio	5,500,000	—
Total	6,000,000	—	Total	7,500,000	$1,500,000
Net worth	$6,000,000	**0% debt ratio**	Net worth	$6,000,000	**20% debt ratio**
		Income Perspective			
Portfolio income	6%	$240,000	Portfolio income	6%	$330,000
After-tax cost of debt	2%	—	After-tax cost of debt	2%	(30,000)
Net income		$240,000	Net income		$300,000
			Additional income compared to existing		$60,000

- This scenario will generate an extra $60,000 a year of cash flow.
  - This assumes that their portfolio outperforms the cost of debt by 4 percent per year.
- That $60,000 divided by the $4 million represents an additional 1.5 percent rate of return on their portfolio. Another way of saying this is that their return is 25 percent higher in the optimal scenario ($300,000/$240,000).
- All savings and cash earned from this strategy could be rolled into their portfolio, not into paying down their house. All things being equal, their debt ratio will fall over time by at least the same amount as it would have had those funds been directed to paying down the house.
- Over a five-year period, this $60,000 reinvested at the same 6 percent would create an additional $338,225.
- They should consider choosing to overcollateralize the assets pledged for their home financing and to use low-volatility assets

for that pledge. This will greatly reduce the risk of their ever facing a forced margin call; while that risk can't be entirely eliminated, this strategy would come close to achieving that.

- Depending on the composition of their taxable and tax-deferred assets, they likely still qualify for an ABLF of over $1 million and perhaps $2 million or more.
- They are in a great position to use their ABLF for purchases.
- Any time they don't like this strategy, they can pay off the debt associated with it.

Looking forward:

- Future available funds should consider going into their portfolio.
- Particularly with the mortgage and deductions from property taxes in two locations, ordinary income may be much more tax efficient once they stop working and therefore could be deferred now.

  - Let's assume that this family has professional breadwinners with over $400,000 of income. In that case they could consider aggressively maximizing tax-deferred savings strategies.

WHENEVER POSSIBLE AND ALL THINGS BEING EQUAL, CONSIDER CHOOSING A LOWER-RISK PORTFOLIO WITH SOME DEBT OVER HIGHER-RISK PORTFOLIO WITH NO DEBT

You're going to see a regular theme in this appendix: I would rather have a lower-volatility portfolio with some leverage targeting a rate of return that exceeds my cost of debt in the 4 percent to 5 percent range, versus a high-volatility portfolio with no debt.

Scenario 3: Higher Net Worth, Loves Real Estate

The scenario in Table D.3 illustrates a higher net worth situation. This couple has a big family and they love real estate because they greatly enjoy it and use it often—it provides them with a lifestyle that they and their adult children and grandchildren definitely enjoy—and they feel it is a hedge against inflation over time.

Table D.3   Scenario 3: Higher Net Worth, Loves Real Estate

Higher Net Worth—Scenario A			Higher Net Worth—Scenario B		
Assets		Liabilities	Assets		Liabilities
Real estate			Real estate		
Home	$ 1,000,000	—	Home 2	$ 1,000,000	$ 500,000
Home 2	3,000,000			3,000,000	2,000,000
Investments			Investments		
Portfolio	7,000,000	—	Portfolio	9,500,000	—
Total	11,000,000	—	Total	13,500,000	$2,500,000
Net worth	$11,000,000	**0% debt ratio**	Net worth	$11,000,000	**19% debt ratio**
		Income Perspective			
Portfolio income	6%	$420,000	Portfolio income	6%	$570,000
After-tax cost of debt	2%	—	After-tax cost of debt	2%	(50,000)
Net income		$420,000	Net income		$520,000
			Additional income compared to existing		**$100,000**

In the base case, the couple has an investment portfolio worth $7 million and they have a $1 million primary home up north and a $3 million second home. This scenario would work out exactly the same if, for example, they had a $3 million primary home in Los Angeles and a $1 million ski home in the mountains. Their total net worth is $11 million.

In the base case, the couple chooses to not have any debt. Under the optimal scenario (Scenario B), the client may choose the following:

- 50 percent loan versus their primary residence.
- $2 million loan versus the $3 million value in their second home.

Optimal breakdown: Here what we see is $13.5 million of assets and $2.5 million of liabilities:

- Their net worth is $13.5 million − $2.5 million = $11 million.
- $2.5 million divided by $13.5 million gives a debt ratio of 18.5 percent (rounded up to 19 percent).
- Notice that because their debt is structured against their two homes, they have no risk of a forced margin call due to market movement.
- The appreciation or depreciation of the real estate that they would have over time is independent of the financing in place around those assets.
- Should either of their homes decline in value, they remain in a positive equity position through a 20 percent correction:
  - For example, $3 million − 20 percent correction = $2.4 million property − $2 million loan = $400,000 of equity in the more expensive property.
  - This impact is independent of the financing they have in place around the asset.
- If their portfolio generates an extra 4 percent over their cost of debt, they would have an extra $100,000 a year of income.
  - This would be equal to increasing the return of the portfolio in Scenario A by 1.4 percent net of fees.
- At any point in time if the strategy isn't working for them, they can change it by simply stepping in and paying down their debt.
- Since only a limited amount of money, or no money, would be pledged to secure the home loans, this couple would have a line of credit that would be 35 percent larger and likely at the very desirable interest rate for lines over $5 million.

Looking forward:

- Income and funds generated from their overall strategy should go to their portfolio, not to pay down their strategic debt.

Scenario 4: Ultra-High Net Worth Family

Here we have the situation of a still higher net worth family represented in Table D.4. Statistically speaking, this scenario may not apply to a lot of families or individuals, but reviewing the strategies appropriate

Table D.4   Scenario 4: Ultra-High Net Worth

Ultra-High Net Worth—Scenario A			Ultra-High Net Worth—Scenario B		
Assets		**Liabilities**	**Assets**		**Liabilities**
Real estate			Real estate		
Home	$ 5,000,000	—	Home 2	$ 5,000,000	$ 3,000,000
Home 2	5,000,000			5,000,000	3,000,000
Investments			Investments		
Portfolio	20,000,000	—	Portfolio	30,000,000	4,000,000
Total	30,000,000	—	Total	40,000,000	$10,000,000
Net worth	$30,000,000	**0% debt ratio**	Net worth	$30,000,000	**25% debt ratio**
		Income Perspective			
Portfolio income	6%	$1,200,000	Portfolio income	6%	$1,800,000
After-tax cost of debt	2%	—	After-tax cost of debt	2%	(200,000)
Net income		$1,200,000	Net income		$1,600,000
			Additional income compared to existing		**$ 400,000**

to those in the higher net worth range—sometimes called ultra-high net worth—can provide important insights for those at all levels of investing.

In the base case, the family owns a $5 million primary home and a $5 million second home, and they have an investment portfolio of $20 million for a net worth of $30 million. Many such families may feel as though they do not need additional income, and that their home or homes may protect them from inflation and potential weakness in the dollar. (The idea here is that if one's local currency—in this case, the dollar—falls by a great deal, high-end homes hold value as foreigners step in to buy, which indeed has historically been the case in some situations.)

ULTRA-HIGH NET WORTH INVESTORS ALSO TEND TO LACK A DEBT STRATEGY

You might be surprised to find out that based on my professional experience, high net worth, higher net worth, and even ultra-high net worth investors have something in common with average investors—they usually do not have any inkling about Strategic Debt Philosophy. What I've seen time and again is that they, too, tend to either be far too highly leveraged, or they are completely debt averse. Here, too, I would urge these individuals and families to seek an optimal middle ground.

Many feel that in a worst-case scenario they could sell their home for around 30 percent less than it is worth, or in this case, for around $3.5 million, which would provide plenty of flexibility, especially considered on a relative basis as the world at large would be in much worse shape. Along the way—and if there is never an emergency need to sell it—the family gets to enjoy a great home. They recognize they are taking some risks here but feel that they have similar risks with regard to their other assets without those other assets providing the same lifestyle benefits. Similarly, second homes also have a utility aspect to them that a municipal bond portfolio, for example, just does not offer. I'm not saying that I totally agree with this thinking, but I am saying that a lot of people do implement this type of a philosophy (or justification).

Now, since this family's net worth is $30 million, they could say that they don't want to have any debt, as shown in Scenario A. But let's look at a more optimal Scenario B for them. They could

- Structure their balance sheets so that they had $3 million of debt versus each of the homes
- Leverage their core portfolio by $4 million
  - This could be accomplished over time by paying for their taxes, cars, improvements and renovations to their properties, and so on, through their ABLF.

- Their net worth is $40 million − $10 million = $30 million.
  - Again, net worth will never change based on financing.
- $10 million divided by 40 million is a 25 percent debt ratio.
  - Notice that 25 percent ($10 million) of their balance sheet is in residential real estate and the other 75 percent ($30 million) could be in a globally diversified portfolio comprised of all assets that one can invest in.
- In Scenario B they will generate approximately $400,000 a year of excess income.
  - That is a 33 percent greater return than the base case Scenario A.
  - It is equal to increasing the return of Scenario A by 2 percent per year on a net basis.
- They will gain considerable tax benefits.
- Anytime they don't like their strategic debt strategy, they can pay off their debt.

ADVANCED APPLICATIONS

The asset in the preceding scenario is listed as "portfolio," but this portfolio would likely be comprised of multiple assets. The $4 million on the ABLF could be the equity component to an investment in a closely held business, real estate, farm, private equity, or other venture.

Depending on the asset in which you are investing, it may be eligible for additional leverage. Some of this leverage may be available nonrecourse (where you do not have a personal guarantee). The combination of recourse and nonrecourse assets leads to more advanced debt ratio calculations.

For now I will just point out that throughout your life you have likely seen high net worth people go through very public bankruptcies yet continue on with their life. For example, there are billionaires who own companies that went bankrupt but the people continue to be on the billionaire list. This is often accomplished by not only using a debt philosophy, but also by implementing clear lines between recourse and nonrecourse.

Is there another alternative for this family? After presenting Strategic Debt Philosophy and Practices to a client, I'll often hear something like the following: "Tom, these are neat ideas, but personally, I'm much more concerned with protecting the downside versus having additional upside." How could we apply the ideas found in this book with this goal in mind?

For one thing, this family could reach for a lower yield with the levered portfolio and target the same income!

Compare this with Scenario 5.

Table D.5 shows that the optimal scenario has a lower required rate of return to accomplish the same income objective. This thinking

Table D.5   Scenario 5: Ultra-High Net Worth—Same Income on a Lower Return with Debt

Alternate Returns					
Ultra-High Net Worth—Scenario A			**Ultra-High Net Worth—Scenario B**		
Assets		**Liabilities**	**Assets**		**Liabilities**
Real estate			Real estate		
Home	$ 5,000,000	—	Home 2	$ 5,000,000	$ 3,000,000
Home 2	5,000,000			5,000,000	3,000,000
Investments			Investments		
Portfolio	20,000,000	—	Portfolio	30,000,000	4,000,000
Total	30,000,000	—	Total	40,000,000	$10,000,000
Net worth	$30,000,000	**0% debt ratio**	Net worth	$30,000,000	**25% debt ratio**
Income Perspective					
Portfolio income	6%	$1,200,000	Portfolio income	**4.67%**	**$1,400,000**
After-tax cost of debt	2%	—	After-tax cost of debt	2%	(200,000)
Net income		$1,200,000	Net income		**$1,200,000**
			Additional income compared to existing		—

can be applied to each of the scenarios previously gone through in this appendix.

Never Pay Down Debt?

In the conclusion, we suggested the paradoxes of an optimal debt ratio. Here are some forward-looking balance sheets that put some math around some of these previously discussed ideas.

In all cases we assume

- An investment growth rate of 6 percent.
- Real estate growth rate of 2 percent.

In the first case, shown in Table D.6, the investors leave their debt constant, that is, they pay the interest only and direct the rest of their savings to their portfolio. Notice how over a 10-year period, their debt ratio declines from 32 percent to 17 percent, and 10 years from now they have a net worth of $7.1 million ($8.6 million of assets − $1.5 million of liabilities = $7.1 million).

Table D.7 illustrates what would happen if the investors aggressively paid off their debt. At the end of 10 years they would have a balance sheet comprised of $6.6 million in assets and no debt, so a leverage ratio of 0 percent.

In this example the investors who paid down their debt have $477,119 less after 10 years compared to the investors who focused on building a portfolio with an optimal debt ratio!

With the assumptions in the preceding analysis, $477,119 represents the maximum possible gain as it assumes zero savings associated with the repayment of the debt over time. For example, if I paid down $150,000 of debt in the first year and the interest rate on that debt was 4 percent, I would save $6,000 each year for the next 10 years. This would continue each year.

This has been shown this way to best illustrate the mathematical proof that *your rate of return on paying down debt is exactly equal to your after-tax cost of that debt.* Therefore, the goal of the Investors is to minimize the rate and to maximize the tax benefits. Anytime they don't like where the rate is versus their investment options—or should

Table D.6 Future Value, Maintain Debt

Future Value—Maintain Debt

	1	2	3	5	7	10
Real Estate Growth Rate	2%					
Investment Growth Rate	6%					
Real estate	$2,000,000	$2,040,000	$2,080,800	$2,164,864	$2,252,325	$2,390,185
Growth	40,000	40,800	41,616	43,297	45,046	47,804
Ending value	2,040,000	2,080,800	2,122,416	2,208,162	2,297,371	2,437,989
Investments	2,500,000	2,650,000	2,959,000	3,633,732	4,391,862	5,708,318
Growth	—	159,000	177,540	218,024	263,512	342,499
Savings	150,000	150,000	150,000	150,000	150,000	150,000
Ending balance	2,650,000	2,959,000	3,286,540	4,001,756	4,805,373	6,200,817
Total assets	**4,690,000**	**5,039,800**	**5,408,956**	**6,209,918**	**7,102,745**	**8,638,805**
Debt constant	(1,500,000)	(1,500,000)	(1,500,000)	(1,500,000)	(1,500,000)	(1,500,000)
Net worth	**$3,190,000**	**$3,539,800**	**$3,908,956**	**$4,709,918**	**$5,602,745**	**$7,138,805**
Debt ratio	*32%*	*30%*	*28%*	*24%*	*21%*	*17%*

Table D.7 Future Value, Aggressively Pay Off Debt

Future Value—Pay Down Debt

| Real Estate Growth Rate | 2% |
| Investment Growth Rate | 6% |

	1	2	3	5	7	10
Real estate	$2,000,000	$2,040,000	$2,080,800	$2,164,864	$2,252,325	$2,390,185
Growth	40,000	40,800	41,616	43,297	45,046	47,804
Ending value	2,040,000	2,080,800	2,122,416	2,208,162	2,297,371	2,437,989
Investments	2,500,000	2,500,000	2,650,000	2,977,540	3,345,564	3,984,620
Growth	—	150,000	159,000	178,652	200,734	239,077
Savings	—	—	—	—	—	—
Ending balance	2,500,000	2,650,000	2,809,000	3,156,192	3,546,298	4,223,697
Total assets	**4,540,000**	**4,730,800**	**4,931,416**	**5,364,354**	**5,843,669**	**6,661,686**
Debt	(1,500,000)	(1,350,000)	(1,200,000)	(900,000)	(600,000)	(150,000)
Debt pay down	150,000	150,000	150,000	150,000	150,000	150,000
Debt ending balance	**(1,350,000)**	**(1,200,000)**	**(1,050,000)**	**(750,000)**	**(450,000)**	**—**
Net worth	**$3,190,000**	**$3,530,800**	**$3,881,416**	**$4,614,354**	**$5,393,669**	**$6,661,686**
Debt ratio	33%	29%	24%	17%	10%	2%
					Difference	*$477,119*

there be a change in tax laws—they can pay down their debt. They are also seeking investment options that on average, over a 3-, 5-, and 10-year period, can outperform their after-tax cost of debt. As long they capture a positive spread (see Chapter 5), they win. The greater the positive spread, the bigger their win.[1]

BIGGEST LESSON

Many people try to aggressively pay down their debt with a goal of retiring debt free. Before we even factor in the tax benefits, we should consider framing a possibility that this approach is not necessarily optimal. In fact, the greater the need for income from a portfolio, the more paying down debt may limit a family's ability to accomplish this goal, as they are

- Receiving a return exactly equal to their after-tax cost of debt.
- Locking up money in an asset that will appreciate or depreciate regardless of the financing around it.
- Reducing the amount of liquid after-tax dollars they have available.
- Reducing tax benefits.

Notes

1. The information in this appendix is to be considered in a holistic way as a part of the book and not to be considered on a stand-alone basis. This includes, but is not limited to, the discussion of risks of each of these ideas as well as all of the disclaimers throughout the book. The material is presented with a goal of encouraging thoughtful conversation and rigorous debate on the risks and potential benefits of the concepts between you and your advisors based on your unique situation, risk tolerance, and goals.

Glossary*

ABLF: Assets-based loan facility. This is a broad term to represent all types of lines of credit that are secured by assets that are on deposit at financial institutions. It may be a purpose or nonpurpose facility.

amortized loan: Requires the borrower to repay parts of the loan amount over time.

available credit: The amount of credit available on your line of credit or ABLF. This will typically fluctuate according to the value of the assets securing the line.

average cost of capital: Typically called the weighted average cost of capital, or WACC. For firms it is the weighted average cost of a firm's common equity, preferred stock, and debt. Individuals need to apply a similar framework and consider the cost of debt compared to the opportunity cost of equity with their investment decisions.

average tax rate: Tax bill divided by taxable income. This is also called your effective tax rate.

balloon payment: A large final payment on a loan.

call provision: A written agreement between an issuing corporation and its bondholders that gives the corporation the option to redeem the bond at a specified price before the maturity date.

capital structure: The mix of various debt and equity capital maintained by a firm or individual.

collateral: Assets that are pledged as security for payment of debt.

---

*Many of the terms shown here are from (or adapted and applied to the individual from) the glossaries that can be found in: Stephen A. Ross, Randolph Westerfield, and Jeffrey Jaffe, *Corporate Finance*, 10th ed. (New York: McGraw-Hill, 2013); and Ziv Bodie, Alex Kane, and Alan Marcus, *Investments*, 9th ed. (New York: McGraw-Hill, 2011).

correlation: A standardized statistical measure of the dependence of two random variables. Defined as the covariance divided by the standard deviations of the two variables.

cost of debt: The cost of borrowing.

coupon: The stated interest payment on a debt instrument.

coverage ratio: The available credit compared to the amount that has been drawn on a line. Since available credit is a function of assets, this can also be looked at as the percentage drawn relative to the total assets securing an ABLF. The book suggests keeping your draw under 50 percent of your available credit.

debt: Loan agreement that is a liability of the individual. An obligation to repay a specified amount at a particular time.

debt capacity: Ability to borrow. The amount an individual or firm can borrow.

depreciation: A noncash expense reflecting the decreased value of an asset over its estimated useful life.

discount rate: Rate used to calculate the present value of future cash flows.

dividend: Payment made by a firm to its owners from sources other than current or accumulated retained earnings.

effective tax rate: Traditionally defined as your total tax paid/adjusted gross income (AGI). I'd suggest that with the ideas expressed in the book AGI can be deferred (reduced) so you could also look at this as total tax paid/gross income.

endogenous: "From within"; as used in this text it means within your assumptions/things that you have already factored in.

exogenous: "From outside"; as used in this text it describes events that occur that are outside your assumptions/things you didn't factor in.

expected return: Average of possible returns weighted by their probability.

financial distress: Events preceding and including bankruptcy, such as violation of loan agreements.

financial distress costs: For companies, legal and administrative costs of liquidation or reorganization (direct costs). An impaired ability to do business and an incentive toward selfish strategies such as taking large risks, underinvesting, and milking a property (indirect costs).

financial leverage: Extent to which a firm relies on debt.

hedging: Taking a position in two or more securities that are negatively correlated (taking opposite trading positions) to reduce risk.

high-yield bond: Junk bond—a speculative grade bond.

hostile takeover: A takeover that occurs against the wishes of stockholders in the acquired firm.

inflation: A fall in the buying power of a unit of currency.

inflation risk: Risk faced by investors due to uncertainty about future inflation.

interest rate: The price paid for borrowing money.

interest rate risk: The chance that a change in the interest rate will result in an adverse effect on the borrower.

junk bond: A speculative grade bond.

liabilities: Debts of the individual.

LIBOR: London Interbank Offered Rate. It is the rate the most credit-worthy banks charge one another for large loans of Eurodollars overnight in the London market.

line of credit: An agreement that allows individuals to borrow up to a previously specified limit.

liquidity: Refers to the ease and quickness of converting assets to cash. Also called marketability.

long-term debt: An obligation having a maturity of more than one year.

marginal tax bracket: The rate at which incremental ordinary income is taxed.

municipal bonds: Bonds issued by a municipality such as a city or state.

nonpurpose loan: An ABLF that explicitly does not let you buy, carry, or trade securities.

nonqualified money: Money that you have already paid taxes on (think of the money in your investment account, outside of your IRA).

present value: The value of a future cash stream discounted to present day.

purpose loan: An ABLF that enables you to buy securities.

qualified money: Money that you haven't paid taxes on yet/money that is inside tax-deferred programs (IRA, deferred compensation plans, etc.).

rent: A contractual arrangement to grant the use of specific assets for a specified time in exchange for payment.

scenario analysis: Analysis of the effect on a project or investment portfolio of different scenarios with each scenario involving many variable changes.

securities: Tradable financial investments such as stocks, bonds, and derivatives.

sinking fund: In corporate finance, an account managed by the bond trustee for the purpose of repaying the bonds. In your personal life, a separate savings account you establish to cover a known future obligation.

TIPS: Treasury Inflation Protected Securities. U.S. government securities that promise payment in real, not nominal, terms.

volatility: Refers to how volatile a security is, or how likely it is to move substantially up or down in any given time period. This is typically measured by standard deviation.

WACC: Weighted average cost of capital. The weighted average cost of a firm's common equity, preferred stock, and debt.

Bibliography

R eaders who wish to familiarize themselves with the corporate finance and investment themes in this book are encouraged to read the following textbooks:

Ross, Stephen A., Randolph Westerfield, and Jeffrey Jaffe. *Corporate Finance*. 10th ed. New York. McGraw-Hill, 2013.

Bodie, Ziv, Alex Kane, and Alan Marcus. *Investments*. 9th ed. New York: McGraw-Hill, 2011.

■ ■ ■

Ideas from the following papers are indirectly referenced through concepts in this book and directly referenced in the aforementioned textbooks. You are encouraged to read them as well:

Agrawal, Anup, and Nandu Nagarajan. "Corporate Capital Structure, Agency Costs, and Ownership Control: The Case of All Equity Firms." *Journal of Finance* 45 (September 1990): 1325–1331.

Altman, E. I. "A Further Empirical Investigation of the Bankruptcy Cost Questions." *Journal of Finance*, September 1984:1067–1089.

Andrade, Gregor, and Steven N. Kaplan. "How Costly Is Financial (Not Economic) Distress? Evidence from Highly Leveraged Transactions That Became Distressed." *Journal of Finance*, October 1998: 1443–1493.

Bar-Or, Yuval. "An Investigation of Expected Distress Costs." Unpublished paper, Wharton School, University of Pennsylvania, March 2000.

Barberis, Nicholas, and Richard Thaler. "A Survey of Behavioral Finance." In *The Handbook of the Economics of Finance*, ed. G. M. Constantinides, M. Harris, and R. Stulz (Amsterdam: Elsevier, 2003): 1053–1158.

Bris, Auturo, Ivo Welch, and Ning Zhu. "The Costs of Bankruptcy: Chapter 7 Liquidation versus Chapter 11 Reorganization." *Journal of Finance*, June 2006: 1253–1303.

Cutler, David M., and Lawrence H. Summers. "The Costs of Conflict Resolution and Financial Distress: Evidence from the Texaco—Penzoil Litigation." *Rand Journal of Economics*, Summer 1988: 157–172.

Graham, John. "How Big Are the Tax Benefits of Debt?" *Journal of Finance*, 2000: 1901–1942.

Graham, John, and Campbell Harvey. "The Theory and Practice of Corporate Finance." *Journal of Financial Economics*, May/June 2001:187–243.

Kahneman, D., and A. Tversky. "Prospect Theory: An Analysis of Decision under Risk." *Econometrica* 47 (1979): 263–291.

Lubben, Stephen J. "The Direct Costs of Corporate Reorganization: An Empirical Examination of Professional Fees in Chapter 11 Cases." *American Bankruptcy Law Journal*, 2000: 509–522.

Markowitz, Harry. "Portfolio Selection." *Journal of Finance*, March 1952: 77–91.

Meyers, S. C. "The Capital Structure Puzzle." *Journal of Finance* 39 (July 1984): 574–592.

Miller, Merton. "Debt and Taxes." *Journal of Finance*, May 1977: 261–275.

Modigliani, F., and M. Miller. "The Cost of Capital, Corporation Finance and the Theory of Investment." *American Economic Review* 48, no. 3 (1958): 261–297.

Modigliani, F., and M. Miller. "Corporate Income Taxes and the Cost of Capital: A Correction." *American Economic Review* 53, no. 3 (1963): 433–443.

Warner, J. B. "Bankruptcy Costs: Some Evidence." *Journal of Finance*, May 1997: 337–347.

Weiss, Lawrence A. "Bankruptcy Resolution: Direct Costs and Violation of Priority Claims." *Journal of Financial Economics* 27 (1990): 285–314.

White, M. J. "Bankruptcy Costs and the New Bankruptcy Code." *Journal of Finance*, May 1983: 477–488.

About the Author

Tom Anderson has his MBA from the University of Chicago and a BSBA from Washington University in St. Louis, where he achieved a double major in Finance and International Business. During his undergraduate years Tom studied abroad extensively, participating in programs at the London School of Economics and the Cass Business School at City University London, and he spent a full year at ESCP Europe on their Madrid campus.

In 2002, Tom attended the Wharton School of the University of Pennsylvania and subsequently obtained the title of Certified Investment Management Analyst (CIMA), sponsored by the Investment Management Consultants Association (IMCA). In addition, Tom has earned the Chartered Retirement Planning Counselor (CRPC) designation through the College for Financial Planning.

Tom worked in investment banking in New York before moving into private wealth management. He is fluent in Spanish and has lived and worked in Spain and Mexico. His extensive academic studies at some of the top schools in finance and economics, international experiences, and institutional background deliver a unique perspective on global markets.

Tom has received multiple national recognitions for his wealth management accomplishments including being named three times by Barron's Magazine as one of America's Top 1,000 advisors: State by State. He is married and lives with his wife and three children in Chicago.*

About the Companion Website

This book includes a companion website, which can be found at www.wiley.com/go/thevalueofdebt. The site contains a debt calculator that is organized similar to the case studies in Chapter 5 and Appendix D.

Readers naturally try to apply the themes of this book to their personal balance sheet—that's the goal! Using this calculator you can input a rough sketch of your current assets and liabilities. The calculator will give you some feedback on your current amount of debt (above or below the optimal range). It will then enable you to run a side-by-side comparison with another balance sheet.

The tool is designed to encourage thought and discussion; it is not designed to deliver individual solutions. Incorrect application of the ideas in this book and website can have serious consequences. Further, you may very well have unique risks or costs of financial distress in your life that lowers your optimal debt ratio range. You may be victim of the behavioral finance issues we discussed, including an inability to handle the responsibility that comes with debt and/or be unwilling to understand the central premise of this book: It is not about buying things you cannot afford; it is about better ways to finance and pay for the things that you can afford.

There are many, many inputs in determining your individual optimal debt ratio, and that number may very well change throughout your life. You should therefore use the calculator as a starting place to trigger meaningful conversations with your CPA, private banker, and financial advisors. Please have them verify that the information you have input is correct, and please visit with them for a complete discussion about your individual situation before taking any action.

To receive these free benefits, visit the website at www.wiley.com/go/thevalueofdebt. When prompted for a password, please enter "get-advice."

Index